PRINCETON
MIDDLE EASTERN SOURCES IN TRANSLATION

M. Şükrü Hanioğlu, Editor

Chinese Travelers to the
Early Turkish Republic

Chinese Travelers
to the
Early Turkish Republic

Giray Fidan

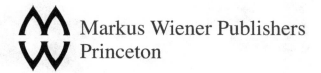

Markus Wiener Publishers
Princeton

For information write to:
Markus Wiener Publishers
231 Nassau Street, Princeton, NJ 08542
www.markuswiener.com

Library of Congress Cataloging-in-Publication Data

Names: Fidan, Giray, 1980- editor, translator.
Title: Chinese travelers to the early Turkish republic / edited and
    translated by Giray Fidan.
Other titles: Princeton series of Middle Eastern sources in translation.
Description: Princeton, New Jersey : Markus Wiener Publishers, 2018. |
    Series: Princeton series of Middle Eastern sources in translation |
    Includes bibliographical references.
Identifiers: LCCN 2018041453| ISBN 9781558766358 (hardcover : alk. paper) |
    ISBN 1558766359 (hardcover : alk. paper) | ISBN 9781558766365 (pbk. : alk.
    paper) | ISBN 1558766367 (pbk. : alk. paper)
Subjects: LCSH: Turkey—Description and travel. |
    Chinese—Travel—Turkey—History—20th century. | Travelers--China. |
    Travelers—Turkey. | Turkey—Relations—China. | China—Relations—Turkey.
Classification: LCC DR428 .C47 2018 | DDC 956.1/01540923951—dc23
LC record available at https://lccn.loc.gov/2018041453

Markus Wiener Publishers books are printed in the United States of America on acid-free paper, and meet the guidelines for permanence and durability of the Committee on Production Guidelines for Book Longevity of the Council on Library Resources.

To my grandmother Necla

Contents

Acknowledgements ix
Abbreviations x
Introduction xi

CHAPTER 1
Sao Ke Alfred Sze and His Travel Notes on Turkey 1

CHAPTER 2
Hu Hanmin: A Quest for a Way Out 25

CHAPTER 3
Ankara: The New Capital of Turkey 63

CHAPTER 4
He Yaozu on Turkey 71

CHAPTER 5
The Turkish Diary of Hu Shiqing 85

Glossary 120
Notes 128
About the Editor and Translator 130

Acknowledgements

This book is the product of my research project conducted at Princeton University. I am grateful to William M. Blair and Tarek Elsayed from the Near Eastern Studies Department for their great friendship, support, discussions and conversations. My special thanks go to Martin Heijdra for helping and instructing me all the time at the East Asian Library and Amy Wang for initial editing of the book. Finally, I extend my gratitude to my sponsor Michael A. Reynolds for his kind guidance, help and support.

Abbreviations

BCA = Başbakanlık Cumhuriyet Arşivi (Prime Ministry Republican Archives), Ankara

BOA = Başbakanlık Osmanlı Arşivi (Prime Ministry Ottoman Archives), Ankara"

JSSDAG = Jin Shi Suo Dang An Guan (Institute of Modern History Archives, Academia Sinica), Taipei

Introduction

Chinese interest in distant Anatolia or Turkey dates back to the early stages of Chinese written histories. As early as the Han dynasty there were accounts of remote western territories such as Iran and Anatolia. During the early times, Chinese perceptions were mostly dependent on second-hand information gathered mostly from emissaries or merchants arriving in China for diplomatic and trade relations. Up until the age of exploration, there were accounts of "Rum," or "Rumi,"[1] namely the Ottoman Empire, in Chinese historical records such as those from the Yuan and Ming dynasties. The interest in Turkey became even more significant by the end of the nineteenth century due to the modernization efforts taking place in the Ottoman Empire. Not only were intellectuals such as Kang Youwei, Liang Qichao[i] and Hu Hanmin keen to understand the developments and reforms in the Ottoman Empire but so was the Qing government. In an archival document dated 1909, a Qing government diplomat in Paris wrote a letter back to Beijing that included a Chinese translation of the 1876 Ottoman constitution.[ii] The famous Kang Youwei also wrote a trav-

---

1. "Rum" and "Rumi" are Turkish pronunciations of the Roman Empire. "Rum" or "Diyar-ı Rum" was also generally applied by Ottomans to determine their territories. In Chinese Historical documents, the Ottoman Empire was called "Lu Mei," "Lu Mu" and "Lu Mi" or "Lu Mi Guo" which was also variations of "Rum." See: 马建春， 明嘉靖、万历朝噜嘧铳的传入、制造及使用," 回族研究, no. 04 (2007): 70; Salih Özbaran, *Bir Osmanlı kimliği: 14.–17. yüzyıllarda Rûm/Rûmi aidiyet ve imgeleri* (İstanbul: Kitap Yayinevi, 2004), 42, 54, 100, 102; Cemal Kafadar, "Introduction: A Rome of One's Own: Reflections on Cultural Geography and Identity in the Lands of Rum," *Muqarnas* 24 (2007): 7–25.

elogue about the Ottoman capital Istanbul in 1908, which was published in his *"Bu Ren"* magazine in 1913. His interest in Turkey dates back as early as 1898 when he wrote a special report to Guang Xu, then the emperor of the Qing dynasty. The title of the report was "The Decline of The Turks." In this text, despite some exaggerations and misunderstandings, Youwei underlined the necessity and inevitability of political reforms in China by making use of the Ottoman Empire as an example. Within the document, Youwei implicitly linked himself to the reformist Ottoman vizier Midhat Pasha and urged the emperor to immediately implement reforms in China. Sadly, not long after this report appeared, Youwei had to flee from China and lived in exile from 1898 until the birth of the Republic of China in 1912. While he was in exile, Youwei arrived in Istanbul via Romania just three days after the 1908 Young Turk Revolution, which restored the 1876 Constitution. His accounts of the Ottoman capital also show differences between his positive take on the Young Turks in 1898 and his skepticism over the new constitution and reforms after seeing the situation on the ground in Istanbul; his newer writings, which turned out to be mostly right underlined the shortcomings and predicted the obstacles ahead.

The Ottoman state was keen to modernize. On the other hand, the Chinese state was not. Ottomans, from the sultan to the ruling elite, recognized the inevitability of reforms, and their awareness of the impulses of westernization came earlier than that of the Chinese.

With the outbreak of the War of Independence in Turkey, Chinese interest in Turkish nation-building began to rise. There is no doubt that the Kuomintang, the Chinese Nationalist Party, was very interested in Turkish affairs, and Chinese communists understood the importance of Turkish independence efforts against foreign forces. The first Chinese Communist bulletin, the *Guide*, published several articles advocating Turkish independence and supporting the independence struggle. The *Guide* started its publication in Shanghai, China, in September 1922 and was one of the earliest newspapers run by the Communist Party of China. This weekly bulletin appeared each Wednesday with about 12,000 (later 20,000) words in each issue. Because the *Guide* opposed capitalism, its publication and sale was banned in Shanghai, after which it moved to Beijing, Guangzhou, Wuhan, and other cities. By the time the bulletin ceased its publication on July 18, 1927, with its 201st issue, it had a great impact upon China's modern history. One of the articles discussed below is "Wish Turkish Nationalist Party Victory," written by Cai Hesen, one of China's most famous Marxist theorists in the early twentieth century. He was the first editor-in-chief of the *Guide* and remained in that position from 1922 to 1925. The second article included is "The International Value of Turkish Nationalist Army's Victory" by Gao Junyu, whose published pen name was Junyu. Both of these articles reflect the Chinese Communist perception of and opinion on the Turkish War of Independence.

Wish Turkish Nationalist Party Victory[iii]

In the last century, no countries were more oppressed internationally than Turkey and China. The problem of Turkey and China is in essence the so-called problem of the Near East and Far East. These two places end up in, on one hand, the center of the international imperial war of insatiable appetite, and on the other, the most bitterly exploited and oppressed region where one third of the mankind lives. Before 1914, imperial powers had brought all similar evils to Turkey as to China: military oppression, land division, blackmail for compensation, financial manipulation, extraterritoriality, incitement of civil strife, and the creation of national enmity by promoting Christian ideology and accusing the Muslims as a barbarian and exclusive group. Due to imperialist powers, Turkey fell apart and crawled with chains on, losing the competence to start afresh. What's worse, they manipulated the ruling class and the parties, turning them into their servants as either Anglophile or Germanophile. As a result, Turkey got caught in the bloody whirlpool of the First World War from 1914 to 1918. As the war ended and Germany lost to the Entente countries, Ferid Pasha, the leader of the Anglophiles, came into office by taking the place of the Germanophile Young Turks, tacitly consenting to the exploitation of Britain and France. In August 1920, Turkey was forced to sign with the Entente countries the Treaty of Sevres: it lost two thirds of its land and half of its people to Greece and accepted the imperialist escrow or condominium; its finances were to be controlled by Britain, France, and Italy, and its financial representatives, losing the right to vote, were subject to imperialist counsel; and extraterritoriality expanded. Unfortunately, the dying Istanbul government and Anglophiles thought it impossible to avoid partitioning, and thus submitted itself to the situation. On the one hand, they followed cautiously the words of Britain and on the other hand, they tried hard to please America, which was already fighting for Mesopotamia's oil with Britain. They were still anchoring the hope on internal strife among gangsters, without knowing their single and similar intention of robbery. The treaty ultimately led to four years of a bloody war. Exhausted, the public stood up against the bully. The great and revolutionary-minded General Kemal, with his nationalist party, launched the war in Ankara and organized the new government and the nationalist army, which fought with the Greek army in the west, the British army in the east, and the French army in the south. The nationalist army won fight after fight, changing the situation in Turkey. When Turkey had been badly broken and partitioned, what support and policies did the nationalist party hold onto to assure the victory over the international imperialism? First, it had the support of the oppressed people. Second, it had the diplomatic policy of changing various parties' pro-imperialism stance and the determination to join hands with the similarly-oppressed Soviet Russia. Since 1917 when Soviet Russia was born and became a reliable savior instead of an imperialist demon, it came to the rescue of the oppressed groups worldwide. In the autumn of 1918, Muslim nationalities held a congress in Moscow to stand against the oppression from the Entente countries and to settle internal disagreements among themselves; and at the congress, they and the Soviet government jointly set up a Muslim liberation ally. In the autumn of 1919, the second congress was convened to cement the cooperation. In 1921, Turkey, Persia, Afghanistan, and Soviet Russia signed an even more valuable agreement where unfair imperialist treaties were to be resisted, and the Soviets recognized the complete independence of Muslim countries and agreed to assist them. With the help of Soviet Russia, the Turkish nationalist party defeated the Entente countries. The Red Flag army would very likely march southward all the way to Syria, India, and Mediterranean. At the same time, a coup was staged in Greece and the former Kaiser's brother-in-law restored the monarchy. The tide had turned against the Entente countries. As a result, in February 1921, they convened the Conference of London and modified the Treaty of Sevres, placing the straits management committee under the permanent control of Turkey, allowing Turkish representatives to attend the extraterritoriality abolishing committee and its representatives in the financial committee to exercise their rights to vote, and returning the sovereignty of Smyrna (the only fine port in Asia Minor) to Turkey but with the presence of the Greek army. Dissatisfied, Greece persuaded the Ankara government to re-declare war. The two sides have kept fighting until recently when Kemal's army defeated the Greek army and took Smyrna back. By the advantages of victory, Kemal intends to achieve complete independence and freedom, reclaiming all the rights and land lost in the battle and returning Turkey to a better situation than before the battle for liberation. Such deeds have not only saved the fate of tens of millions of oppressed Muslims in Turkey and the East but set an example for the oppressed nations worldwide. Therefore, beside the birth of Soviet Russia, the Turkish movement represents another historical cause worth our congratulation.

We congratulate Turkey on this victory, on the future overthrow of the oppression from international imperialism, and the building of a complete, independent, and free nation. Is this great victory possible? We have the confidence to say that: (1) if Turkey still holds onto the public support and the momentum of this victory and encourages the oppressed people to fight ever stronger against the international imperialism; (2) if Turkey remains united with Soviet Russia and unshaken by the Imperial France's hypocritical diplomatic policies, the great victory will come true. Some people argue this sanguine situation in Turkey is to some extent France's due, which I must say is a terrible misunderstanding. French imperialists created the impression that they were helping Turkey against Greece's and Britain's diplomatic policies. They did this only because since the Conference of London, (1) they could not preserve their interests in the Near East against Britain; (2) Greece's former Kaiser restored his reign, and Germany might grow stronger; and (3) Turkey and Soviet Russia have worked together ever closer. It was against France's long-held dream of overthrowing Soviet Russia. In essence, France has always been one of Turkey's executioners. If it hadn't been for the above three reasons, would France have felt any sympathy towards Turkey? If Turks had not had the courage to cooperate with Soviet Russia and lingered between imperialists, Turkey wouldn't have achieved today's success. Moreover, if Turkey's nationalist party was to change its policies, believe in what France says, and distance itself from Soviet Russia, it would lose the public trust and get chained by the imperialist powers. General Kemal is too smart to do this because he knows none of these imperialist powers, France or America, are approachable. He knows that the day Turkey grows attached to France or America, it'll be exploited collectively more harshly if tomorrow Britain compromises with France and America. He knows that coming closer with Soviet Russia will spare Turkey from dangers and assure a real liberation. According to recent news, the cooperation between Turkey and Soviet Russia will survive and undermine France's diplomatic policies. Therefore, we are more convinced that the final great victory of Turkey is around the corner. Here follows the news published on the 20th of this month:

(18th Xianglin News report) News came that General Kemal called Russian representative Qi Jilin (Georgy Chicherin) in Berlin and told him that Ankara Government will discuss Near Eastern problems with the Entente countries and Moscow Government on a rational basis. The road to victory is the union of the oppressed nations with Soviet Russia. This road had not been found until 1914; therefore, even the patriotic Young Turks had gone astray and grown attached to imperialist powers, leaving Turkey at bay. Now we have the great and brave General Kemal. Under his leadership, Turkey is now on the road to a great victory, and even the Young Turks are on this road. The oppressed nations in the Near East are walking out of darkness. What a scene for the oppressed nations in the Far East, especially for the Nationalist Party of China who are in the same position as Turkey's nationalist party and have fought alone against the imperialist oppression over the past three decades!

Dear 400 million compatriots, the oppressed Turks have won the war over imperialist powers! Their nationalist party has taken them to the road to a great victory! As we envy them, we should learn from them: please call for our party [KMT] to join hands with Soviet Russia to fight against the imperialist oppression in China!

Please do not turn a blind eye to Turkey's victory in the Near East!
Long live the victory of the oppressed Turkey!
Long live the union of worldwide oppressed nations with Soviet
    Russia!
Long live the liberation of oppressed nations!

The International Value of Turkish Nationalist Army's Victory[iv]

The victory of the Ankara government army has wiped out the forces of Greece, the proxy of Britain, in Smyrna. This is the biggest event in recent world history for its international value in opening a new chapter for all oppressed nations.

This victory is not the victory of Islam over Christianity, of Asians over Caucasians, or of Asians over Europeans, but the victory of the oppressed Turkey over European imperialist powers, which is evident in the establishment of the anti-western power of the Ankara government. Years of oppression and bullying has left Turkey at its last gasp. Such a Turkey, as the world sees, would not survive the last cut from the Western powers. Even the aspirant Young Turks thought the damage had been done and the last resort might be invoking the protection of imperialist powers. However, after three years of vigorous counter-blows from Kemal's men, here comes the big victory. Regardless of the future, Turkey now has the hope of getting rid of its imperialist oppression. This fact is most inspiring for weak nations in similar situations and at least will inspire the movement in Egypt and India to expand.

Britain is badly affected by this victory. The Paris newspaper tells exactly the truth by calling the failure of Greece as the failure of Britain. After the victory over the Central Powers, Britain has borrowed the power of the Entente and the Greek forces in exploiting and taking advantage of Turkey. Now these advantages are at risk. Britain has obtained the Mesopotamian oil from the hands of America to develop its imperialism; and it promotes "freedom of the Strait of Tartary" for the same reason as promoting "the opening up of Chinese ports" — for the convenience of imperialist exploitation. Britain expands at the expense of weak Oriental nations. Owing to its army, the country has obtained great conveniences all the way "from the Strait of Gibraltar to Hong Kong" but now, all these conveniences are at risk. What matters most is the freedom of navigation through the Strait of Gibraltar, without which Britain will lose the basis of "dancing" in Turkey, the conveniences of free navigation to the east of the Suez Canal and handling of Oriental colonies and weak nations including China. This big risk will certainly scare Great Britain into tears. No doubt Lloyd George was almost ready to launch an attack. The military presence of Britain on the strait might lead to some engagement with the Turkish forces, but full confrontation with them? Impossible. The internal damages brought by the WWI, the awakening of the colonial lands, and the prying eyes of America, France, and Japan do not allow Britain to enter into a military confrontation with Turkey. Even the conditions are set; the people have decided to prevent the war; and they certainly can, as was evidenced by the Russian Revolution. So, Britain has no choice but to accept a peaceful settlement with Turkey.

France has, on one hand, supported the petite-entente, dreaming of hegemony over the continent, and on the other hand, signed bilateral agreements with the Ankara government to repel the British presence in the East. Over the past two years, the Entente Cordiale has been totally broken, and nothing has been left but the growing hostility between France and Britain. This time, Britain suffers a blow from Turkey's victory, which satisfied France. Some people think France's reluctance to help Britain is because of its agreement with the Ankara government. This is not the real case. There is no doubt Soviet aid greatly contributed to Kemal's success. What's more, frantic French politicians are strongly against the radicals' efforts to put the working class in power and to help weak nations get rid of the imperialist oppression. Apparently, France hates to see Ankara victorious. The rise of weak nations means a blow to all imperialist powers. France is no exception. Its temporary refusal to work with Britain is finally attributed to their deep estrangement.

This victory helps all oppressed nations realize that only Soviet Russia is a true friend who can help them with the national liberation.

On the European battlefield, we see two opposite trends: the ongoing vigorous conflicts among the imperialist powers and their collective decline, and the unity between workers and oppressed nations. Judging from Britain's situation after Turkey's victory, these two trends have grown even stronger. Let's celebrate!

The first quarter of the twentieth century witnessed China in turmoil and chaos as were the other parts of the non-Western world. The civilization and the country that had endured more than 4,000 years faced an existential crisis. The country had become a semi-colony, and foreign influence was overwhelming. In the wake of the new century, Chinese politicians, intellectuals, and travelers were trying to find a way out of the crisis—a quest to find a way to "save the country." Turkey, having been invaded by foreign powers, and having successfully fought its War of Independence against foreign invading forces and renegotiated unfair treaties, adapted itself to the modern world in the wake of the twentieth century and initiated a series of comprehensive reforms. Turkey became a country of interest for Chinese intellectuals and politicians beginning with the constitutional movements through the early 20th century. For Chinese intelligentsia, Turkey demonstrated a precious model—a country very similar to China with successful experiences. In order to save their own country, they turned their faces to the new Republic of Turkey. This book aims to shed light on Chinese perceptions of the Republican Turkey through Chinese and Turkish archival materials, newspapers, and travel accounts.

CHAPTER 1

Sao Ke Alfred Sze
and his Travel Notes on Turkey

A Brief Biography of Sao Ke Alfred Sze (Shi Zhaoji)

Sao Ke Alfred Sze was the first ambassador of the Republic of China
to the United States of America and was an outstanding diplomat and
politician of the Republican China. He was born on October 4, 1877,
in southern China's Jiang Su Province, received a Western-style education, and studied foreign languages and modern science. In 1892,
when he was 15 years old, he was selected as the interpreter for the
Qing Dynasty's ambassador to the USA. In 1896, he started studying
at Cornell University in the USA. Meanwhile, he was still working
for the Qing Embassy. In 1899, he attended the Hague Convention
as a member of the Chinese delegation. By 1901, he graduated from
Cornell University and, in 1902, went back to China. Between 1902
and 1907 he acted as the head of the Chinese overseas student com-
munities and compiled several books on Western political thought.
In 1907, he was responsible for the railroads in Jilin province. A little
later, he was nominated to the Ministry of Foreign Affairs. [v]

Not long after 1911, with the new Republican government, he was
appointed as the Minister of Transportation by the president of the

Republic of China, Yuan Shi Kai, in 1912.[vi, vii] By 1914, the First World War broke out, and Sao Ke Alfred Sze was appointed as the first ambassador of the Republic of China to the USA, but because of the obstacles in the republican parliament, his post was changed to the UK. He arrived in London by December that same year and remained at the post until 1920. He also attended the Paris Peace Conference in 1919 as a member of the Chinese delegation, along with the Minister of Foreign Affairs of Republic of China. By February 22, 1921, he was appointed as the ambassador to the USA once again, and by March 10 he had arrived in Washington and offered his letter of credence.[viii] In 1923, he was nominated to become the Minister of Foreign Affairs in Zhang Shaozeng's[2] government, though not for long. He resigned and was appointed as the ambassador to the USA once again.[ix]

In 1926, he was offered the post of the foreign ministry seat in Yan Huiqing's government. By June 1928, the government fell when Sao Ke Alfred Sze was the ambassador to Peru. In 1929 he resigned. In the same year, he was appointed the ambassador to the UK and attended the League of Nations as China's representative.[x] In 1933, he was again named the ambassador to the USA, a post he held until August 1935, when he resigned as an ambassador; this was the end of his career as a diplomat. In 1937, he left the USA and returned to China. After his return, he started to work for the resistance against the Japanese invasion. In 1941 he went back to the USA. In April 1945, he attended the San Francisco Conference as a high advisor to the Chinese delegation. In 1948, he was selected as an advisor to the

---

2. Zhang Shaozeng was the premier of Republic of China for a short period in 1923.

International Bank for Reconstruction and Development, a position he held until he resigned in 1950. Between 1941 and 1958, he settled in the USA and passed away in Washington in April 1958.[xi]

Comments on the travel notes of Turkey

Sao Ke Alfred Sze was the second Chinese scholar who went to Turkey after the establishment of the new Republic in 1923. While other Chinese travelers and intellectuals, such as Kang Youwei, Liang Qichao, and Hu Hanmin, had written about Turkey before 1923, Sao Ke Alfred Sze's travel account about the Turkish Republic is the first example of its kind. The travel notes were compiled from his speech at a committee of the Ministry of Foreign Affairs meeting.[xii] The travel account was published in four different journals and the popular newspaper *Shen Bao* (Shun Pao)[xiii], which proves the extent of Chinese interest in Turkey. The travel account of Sao Ke Alfred Sze lacks details, but it is a valuable source for understanding a senior Chinese diplomat's perception of Turkey in the 1920s.

If one thinks of the hardships of traveling from the USA to Turkey in the mid 1920's, Sao Ke Alfred Sze taking such a long journey to Turkey indicates his interest in the country. One of the most surprising discoveries in the notes is that the name of Mustafa Kemal and the other important political figures of Turkey are never mentioned in the text. The country is portrayed without mentioning any political figures. It is impossible that he did not know the leading personalities of the country. This approach is entirely different from the other Chinese scholars who traveled to or wrote about Turkey.

For Sao Ke Alfred Sze, the economic point of view was vital. He repeatedly underlined the abolition of the capitulations, privileges granted by the Ottoman Empire to subjects of foreign states. According to archival material from 1925, just before he traveled to Turkey, he was trying to solve the issue of an unfair treaty—a treaty with the USA—and was also on a quest for solutions to revise or even cancel it.[xiv] The Turkish leadership even gave up some parts of the "Misak-ı Milli" (The National Pact), which meant relinquishing territory, for the sake of eliminating the capitulations. International law and the unfair treaties between major powers and other countries was an important issue for diplomats.

The Republican Archives of Turkey holds one document about Sao Ke Alfred Sze from 1926. According to the document, he was welcomed as an important guest and that he was presented with a signed photograph of Prime Minister İsmet Pasha.[xv] During that period, the exchange of signed photos was an important tool of diplomacy. A signed photo of Chang Kai Shek—along with the signed photos of other historical figures of the time—is now in the museum section of Atatürk's Mausoleum in Ankara.

The texts of the travel notes published in all the magazines and the *Shen Bao* newspaper mentioned above are the same. *Shen Bao* provided the text used for this translation.

Travel Notes on Turkey[xvi]

I went to Turkey; it was in the second half of 1925, and it was the most exciting journey of my [entire] life. Today I am looking forward to talking about it in depth to allow [you], the gentlemen, to understand the current situation. The problems of China and Turkey are very similar; these are the issues that my humble self cannot help but to feel and think deeply on. How did Turkey, which paid a high price, overcome and vanquish these problems? How can China overcome its problems? How can China be compared to Turkey? Now my humble self would like to discuss these questions with the gentlemen. [First], I would like to discuss how I went to the new capital of Turkey, Ankara. These are going to be my statements. If among the gentlemen, there is anyone who wishes to go to Turkey, or anyone who wants to raise questions, or anyone who wishes to understand, please step forward. Your humble servant will talk in details. Recently established Turkey, its people, and their way of handling issues are a splendid example and a reflective mirror for our country. Therefore, I would like to talk about my trip took place in September 1925. My journey started from the USA to Turkey. During that time, the Lausanne Treaty still did not have the approval of the United States Senate. Consequently, US-Turkey diplomatic relations had not yet resumed; Turkey did not have any diplomatic representatives in the US. I was holding a passport for traveling to Turkey; I went to London and tried to obtain a visa from the Turkish Embassy in the UK. I wrote a letter to introduce myself to the Minister of Foreign Affairs of Turkey, immediately went to Venice via Paris and took the Orient Express to arrive in Constantinople[3]; in between I stayed 24 hours in Belgrade and Sofia. When travelers arrive at the Turkish border, two inspectors inspect the passports and baggage. They also opened and examined my baggage, though they did not [actually] examine the luggage, only opened it. They were possibly expressing that I did

---

3. Constantinople, the former name of the capital city of the Ottoman Empire; now called Istanbul.

not have diplomatic seniority within the Turkish borders. Therefore, they were exercising their right to inspect. However, the inspectors' attitudes were very respectful. When talking about Turkey's ban on foreign nationals, with my experience and as an observer, I can tell you, gentlemen, that at present the foreigners, who leave for Turkey with their passports and visas are only allowed [to stay] in Constantinople. If one wishes to stay more than two weeks, one has to obtain a permit from the police station and, before leaving the city, must inform the police. In the case of someone wanting to go to any place in Turkey other than Constantinople, one should obtain a special permit issued by the police authority, and one should submit it when on the train. Furthermore, before leaving any railway station, one has to apply for this permit. Turkey, by implementing such measures, intends to strictly control foreigners and to prevent [foreign] plots. Additionally, they can prevent foreigners from going to some places, so they ban traveling. Moreover, [by doing so], they protect the foreigners, and it is also convenient. The intent behind the current Turkish policy is obvious. Formerly, the policy of foreign powers towards Turkey practiced every kind of restrictions to the country, [so] the Turks gnashed their teeth and did not forget. Therefore, by adopting the policies above, [they are] reformulating a new [sort of] agreement, by being unusually cautious, [they] safeguard their sovereign rights. They fear [that even this] is not satisfactory. Turkey limited the rights of foreigners not only in this way; the more widely known one was to ban foreign news reporters to enter the country. A London-based, well-known newspaper's special correspondent based in Turkey was accused by the Turkish government of creating malice between Turkey and the UK. He was expelled from the country within four hours. Another example was a certain American journalist; after returning to the US for vacation, his visa application was refused. Except for the Russian and Afghan embassies, those of the other countries are still in Constantinople. Every embassy also appointed a secretary to the new Turkish capital city—Ankara. At the same time, the Turkish Ministry of Foreign Affairs also appointed a secretary to Constantinople to communicate conveniently with foreign missions. These representatives are becoming only a body for forwarding documents daily, every embassy—for the negotiations—[even becoming] inferior to the appointed secretaries. In the future, [it seems that] all will move to the new capital city. It is only a matter of time. When I was in Turkey, the organs of the government were still in temporary buildings. The new capital Ankara was developing fast and modern style buildings were being constructed by the Turkish people. Broad streets with pedestrian paths and residential buildings imitating the pictures in American journals were under construction. Ankara is one of the old cities of Turkey; its foundation was approximately in the era of the Spring and Autumn Period.[4] Most of the houses are crumbling, the roads are narrow and crooked, and it is on a rocky highland, difficult to climb from both sides. The new capital is an entirely different place. The old capital city, Constantinople, and the new capital are very different. The former capital possesses ruins in abundance, apparently easy to see, and especially the famous bazaars are quite numerous.[5] The former capital was once in

---

4. Spring and Autumn period of China is from BC 771 to BC 476.

5. Alfred Sze most likely is talking about the numerous bazaars, such as the Grand Bazaar and Spice Bazaar, all around İstanbul.

a prosperous condition; today, it still has the most crowded population, has ancient attractions, and its geographical position is excellent. Yet now, there are many things to preserve. The old and new Turkey are [completely] different, and anyone can understand that at a glance. The Turks are also to be much honored for the construction of a brand-new country. How to develop the new country and how to fulfill this goal is what the Turkish nation has desired for a long time. I talked about the problems of Turkey above; most of these are the same as in China: how to deal with foreign influence, taxes and tariffs, as well as the many economic problems.

My humble opinion is that the problems of Turkey were way worse than China's. In 1919, Turkey's situation was also worse than China's situation 20 years ago. Simply speaking, by the time of the First World War, Turkey's losses were huge, and, after the war, sought peace. Because of the armistice terms, territories of the country were carved up as an award by the Entente. [Turkey] did not dismiss the troops. In Constantinople, the [Entente's] arrogance was everywhere. There were two governments in Turkey: one was the sultan's old government in Constantinople, and the other was the new government of the people of Turkey in Ankara. Regarding foreign affairs, peace negotiations and conditions were undecided. [Most of the] territories of the country were under Coalition Forces' occupation while the Greek Army was under the protection of the Coalition Forces' warships. In İzmir there was an endless invasion. Turkey's problems regarding the foreign intrusion and customs tariffs took twice the time as much as China's and there were also other old and deeply rooted issues. However, with the Turkish nation's determined spirit and the united efforts of the entire country, within three years'

1931, taken from the *Xie Yi Xiao Kan* magazine, No: 3, pp: 21.

Alfred Sze in 1912

1921, in front of the White House

1922, Chinese Embassy in the USA

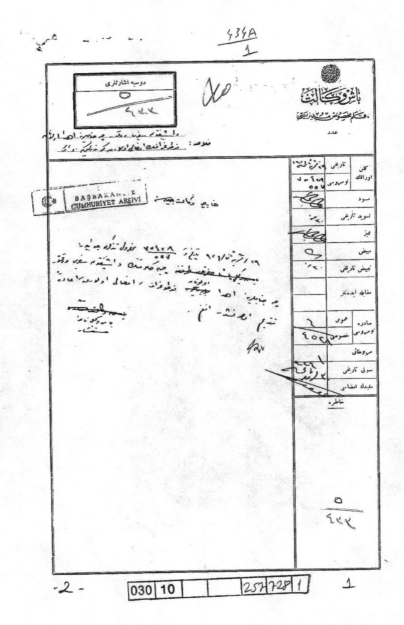

BCA, 30-10-0-0_257-728-1/1
Document regarding a signed photo of [İsmet Pasha] presented to the
Ambassador of the Chinese Government in Washington Mr. Sze.

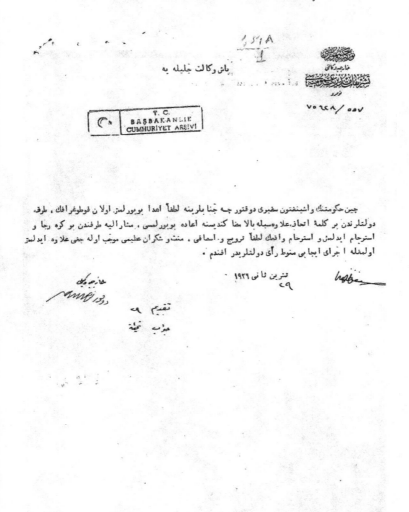

BCA, 30-10-0-0_257-728-1/2
Document regarding the Ambassador of the Chinese Government in
Washington Mr. Sze's accepted the signed photo.

13

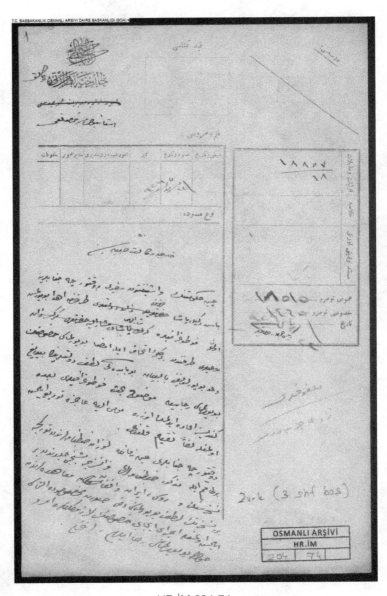

HR.İM 204-74
Ambassador of the Chinese Government in Washington Mr. Sze demanded
a copy of Lausanne treaty negotiations records and copies of the treaties
between Turkey Russia, Iran and Afghanistan.

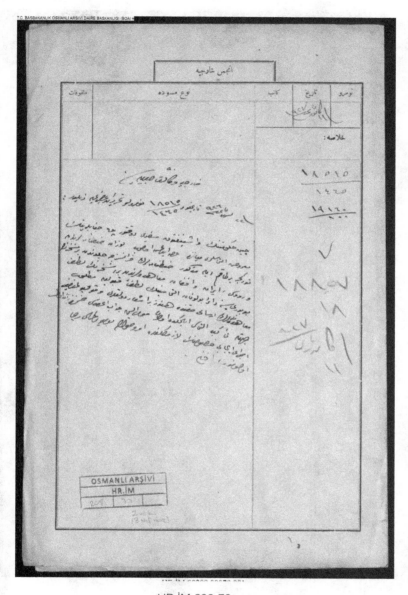

HR.İM 208-70
Regarding sending copies of Lausanne treaty negotiations records and
copies of the treaties between Turkey Russia, Iran and Afghanistan to the
Ambassador of the Chinese Government in Washington Mr. Sze.

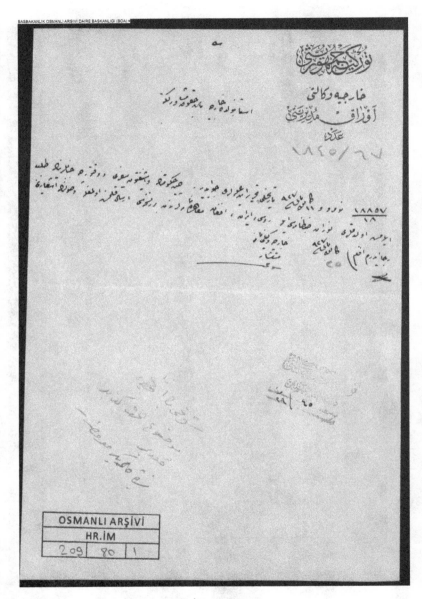

HR.İM 209-80
Copies of Lausanne treaty negotiations records and copies of the treaties
between Turkey Russia, Iran and Afghanistan already sent to the Ambassador
of the Chinese Government in Washington Mr. Sze.

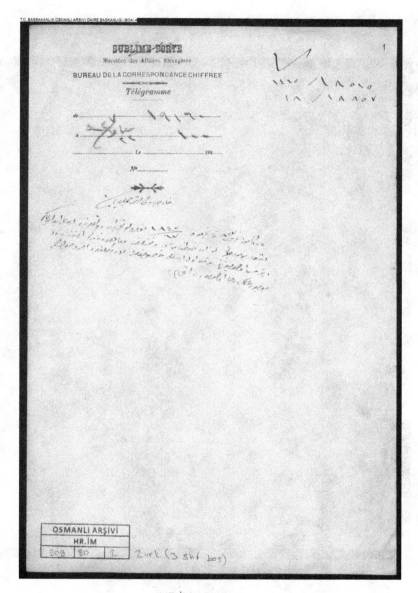

HR.İM 209-80-2
Copies of Lausanne treaty negotiations records and copies of the treaties
between Turkey Russia, Iran and Afghanistan has not been delivered yet to
the Ambassador of the Chinese Government in Washington Mr. Sze.
The urgent sending of documents is demanded.

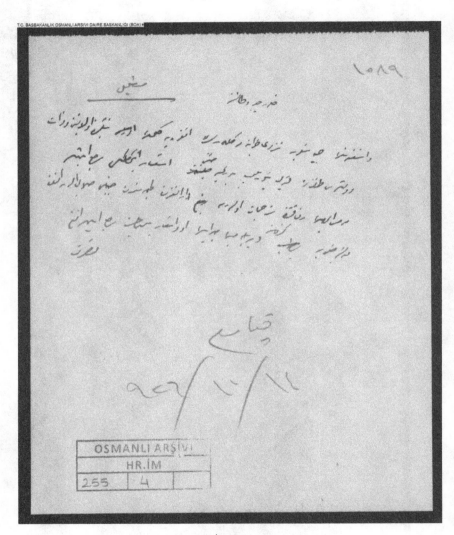

HR.İM 255-4
The Ambassador of the Chinese Government in Washington came and
asked whether it is possible to come to Ankara. A Chinese student from the
Darülfünun [Istanbul University] will be with him as his translator.

HR.İM 255-9

Chinese Ambassador is going to depart for Turkey by 23rd of this month.

time, they unexpectedly drove the Greek Army to the sea and improved their conditions, negotiated the Lausanne Peace Treaty, and set up a strong government in the new capital city. The Entente, also on the terms of the Lausanne Peace Treaty, accepted the abolishment of the unequal privileges[6] enjoyed by foreigners. Herewith Turkey [attempted] to adopt all kinds of measures; details are as follows, and, regarding China, [we] can compare and learn from that example. Instead of the old capital city of Turkey, Constantinople, and the [even] the older capital city, Bursa, Ankara was selected to be the new capital city of the country because of its geographical advantages. Ankara is in the interior and very far from the seaside. The Turks believe constructing the new capital in such a place has three benefits. The first one is the foreign warships; this is a place where it is impossible for warships to attack. Formerly, when Constantinople was the capital city, [if] foreign forces had any demand, they could use warships to reveal their might. Today, there is no such concern. Secondly, the surrounding topography of Ankara easily facilitates defense and prevents an enemy army's invasion. Thirdly, the transportation [to Ankara] is extremely inconvenient, [lacks] accommodation and comfort. Thus foreigners do not want to stay long, and the Nationalist Party[7] members, who are holding the power, can concentrate on their work and, moreover, will be free of interference and

---

6. I.e., the Capitulations.

7. It should be noted that the Chinese, including members of the Communist and Nationalist parties, defined Turkish National forces or the "Kuva-yı Milliye" as the Kuo Min Tang (Guo Min Dang - KMT). In fact, the founding party was called as the Republican People's Party (Cumhuriyet Halk Fırkası, later, Cumhuriyet Halk Partisi, abbreviated as CHP in Turkish. The Communist and the Nationalist Chinese intellectuals must have seen similarities between the Chinese KMT and the Turkish Nationalist movement.

the traps of external factors. Turkey's financial issues [became] quite smoother. By the year 1914, before the outbreak of the First World War, Turkey's most valuable financial resources were all already under foreign control. [Even] the domestic revenues were under the supervision of the Foreign International Debt Committee.[8]

After 1914, the Turkish government regained the control of finances and used the revenue in the first place for the First World War, [mostly] using it for the reorganization of the land forces. The funds were also utilized for the construction of the railways in and around Ankara. In other words, Turkey, although not denying the foreign debt owed, still did not compensate after 1914. So, the issue remained unsettled until June 1928 when the Turkish government and the lenders mapped out a temporary contract for clearing up the debts. Turkey had financial problems, yet the solution for the issue was not like China's [economic] surrender. The most important and notable point of the financial management of Turkey is that the new government was very diligent in handling [economic] affairs and did not take on any foreign debt. The new government of Turkey was deeply aware of the harsh conditions of borrowing money from foreign banks. In the past, borrowers suffered from the harms; today, they [are] sure to keep this in mind and not to forget. Turkey, in trying to handle the capitulations, adopted a resolute policy. At that time, as for the attitude of these countries, there is no need for details [as to why] each country rejected and put forward justifications not to give up their advantageous positions in Turkey. The rejection and arguments were the same as what they put forward in China. Par-

8. In Turkish known as the Düyûn-ı Umûmiye and in English as Ottoman Public Debt Administration.

ticularly, it is astonishing that arguments put forth at the Lausanne Conference from the countries who did not want to give up their advantageous positions were almost the same as Japan's arguments at the 1925 Beijing Conference. The process of how Turkey regained its rights can be summarized as follows: from the beginning, the Turks knew that the Great Powers were not willing to give up their advantageous rights. To regain these rights, Turkey was aware of the necessity of being prepared for great sacrifices. The country was once threatened with war, but Turkey would not bend down, and the [Turks] would fight for the rights of their country [if necessary]. The Turks knew that taking back the capitulations alone would not be sufficient for their [ultimate] goal. During the Great War, the Turks allied with Germany and Austria–Hungary, but when it came to the management of the capitulations problem they responded immediately that [Turkey] should give up these attempts, and [Turkey] agreed. Turkey, since abolishing the capitulations, has witnessed its politics, society, economy, and industry greatly improved. It is evident that capitulations obstruct the development of countries. When I talk to the Turks, as well as foreigners, all of them consider that if the previous system continued or was not revised, the Turkish government could not implement good governance for many years. [Therefore,] as a result of all these major political reforms, it could finally have such [good] results. The foreigners I met in Turkey, some of whom were opposed to the abolition of capitulations at the time, are now all profoundly glad for the abolition of the capitulations. Before their removal, there was constant suspicion and hate between Turks and foreigners. After the abolishment, there is a new kind of friendship and cooperative spirit. In the process of Turkey regaining its rights [from foreign powers], there are still some important points that China should pay particular attention to at present. Foreigners have always advocated for China to have laws that satisfy foreigners in the first place, and then the capitulations could be abolished. With the example of Turkey's experience, the abolishment of the capitulations was in 1923. The [Turks] issued new laws [accordingly,] three years after the abolition. The general situation of Turkey in areas such as agriculture, commerce, art, education, etc., is far less developed compared to China. Commerce and industry are in the hands of Greeks, Armenians, and Jews. Modern education is initiated by foreign missionaries. However, in China, the circumstances [mentioned above] are better to a certain extent. Since ancient times, the Turks always praise their military and have pride for it. In historical context, the Turks are often described as skilled warriors and are capable of sailing through dangerous periods. Perhaps it is this warrior nature of the people and their respect for rules and discipline, loyalty, and obedience that lead them to success. The successful progress of Turkey does not only depend on the efforts of a strong government, [but] also on the contributing force of the people of the entire country. Only if both work together in close cooperation can progress be successful. Moreover, this is what my country can learn from the modern history of Turkey, a reflecting mirror for us. Recent developments in Turkey are as described above. I am humbly confident that Turkey's experience is a significant reference point for our country. There are no countries in the globe whose circumstances are absolutely the same, and the solutions cannot be imitated. The solutions for the problems China faces should be solved according to China's customs. For instance, the Chinese attach importance to common sense and, in the case of disputes, if the counterparty respects justice, the [Chinese] will also be ready to solve the problems according to common sense to reach a peaceful solution. In other words, China is a nation of patience. For its deserved rights, its attitude is always friendly, presenting its arguments on reasonable grounds. It does not want to solve its conflicts with the direct use of military force. This is a clear result if one observes the recent development [in China]. It can clearly be seen that China applies peaceful policies to its problems. However, China, for any rights that are deserved and that it has sworn to obtain, when friendly discussions come out with no results, will never hesitate to take [necessary] unilateral actions.

CHAPTER 2

Hu Hanmin: A Quest for a Way Out

Hu Hanmin was a prominent Chinese politician in the twentieth century. He held many important posts in KMT (Nationalist Party — Kuomintang) governments. His interest in Turkey goes back to the days of the Young Turk revolution, and in 1909 he had written an article on the revolution and used it as a lesson for China.[xvii] His visit to Turkey was a significant one. Later on, when he went back to China, he praised the Turkish experience.[xviii,xix] Sun Ke, Sun Yatsen's son who served as the minister of finance, was also a part of the delegation visiting Turkey.

Hu Hanmin talks about Turkey[xx]

When Hu Hanmin was on his way from Hong Kong to Shanghai, he talked with a newspaper reporter about the Turkish situation. He told us our country and nation could imitate and follow their example. (A gentleman asked him): Mr. Hu had been to Turkey a long time ago. Regarding the recent developments in Turkey, do you have any comments?

(Mr. Hu's reply): The Turkish people are very brave and obedient because Turkey is heavily oppressed. If it was not so, it could not save itself. Everything in the country is neat and well-organized. The people are obedient and united against the outside influences, and the army is now in good condition after the Greco-Turkish war. The men do not wear the Arab red hat (fez), and women do not wear veils. After the government issued an order not to wear these, within 24 hours it was forbidden to wear them. The red hat and the veil are now entirely invisible, and this shows the obedience of the people. The people have an issue which has drawn my attention. They have started investigating the resident registration system (Hukou), where the government orders that on a certain day of a certain month nobody is allowed to go out. People have to obey and remain indoors.[9] Now, the best and the most important thing in Turkey is the unified fiscal system. With the budget reforms, any actions beyond the budget cannot be realized. Every speaker in the country must use the Turkish language; otherwise they cannot deliver speeches. Letters in the postal system also must be written in the Turkish Language; otherwise the postal office will not process and deliver the letter. Letters being sent out of the country must have envelopes addressed in Turkish. The foreign policy of Turkey is based on having no enemies; some may think that weak countries do not have a foreign policy and from time to time may consider war against another country. Everything considered, all institutions and policies of Turkey are indeed consistent with the national behavior. Their KMT (Nationalist Party—i.e., Republican People's Party) is doing very well. They say all of their bureaucrats are Nationalist Party members. I think when you hear that you are all skeptical about that, but their bureaucrats are all KMT party members. They are obedient to all orders and re-

---

9. This was the practice of the census in Turkey for a long period of time.

sponsibilities of the KMT, but they do not have the right to vote. Therefore, these party members have the responsibility but no rights and are not equal members of the party. This method can be described as a strange one.

(Question) The Turkish Revolution was successful, and the Communist Party's power contributed to it significantly, but the Communist Party was later expelled. With regards to the process of the revolution, Turkey is entirely the same with our country. How can Turkey, after expelling the Communist Party, still be consistent internally, while our country could not succeed to do so?

(Answer) In this regard there are two reasons. Firstly, the strong Turkish nationalism promotes unity against foreign forces and influences. Secondly, Turkey has no industrial problems, so there are no major disputes.

Understanding the Experiences and Feelings of New Turkey[xxi]

Regarding the criticism on the two fundamental points of the founding of New Turkey as a country I paid a visit. When I was on a European tour, I went to Turkey to make an observation. Of course, it is not possible to comprehend their real situation entirely, but the things that I heard and saw there generated many thoughts. I did have two doubts about the revival of the Turkish state, and when I met with the minister of education of the new government, I raised these two points. The first question I asked was: "Turkey is now not willing to maintain a religious ideology but will use nationalism to fully replace religion. Can this type of ideology create a singular Islamic

Hu Hanmin, Sun Ke in the Turkish Ministry of Foreign Affairs, Ankara,
March 16, 1928

Hu Hanmin, Sun Ke in front of the National Assembly in Turkish capital Ankara, March 16, 1928

Hu Hanmin in the building of the Embassy of China in Ankara,
March 16, 1928

Hu Hanmin, Sun Ke photo with the soldiers and local people in Ankara, March 16, 1928

Hu Hanmin on a horse carriage in Ankara,
March 16, 1928

Hu Hanmin and Ankara scenery,
March 16, 1928

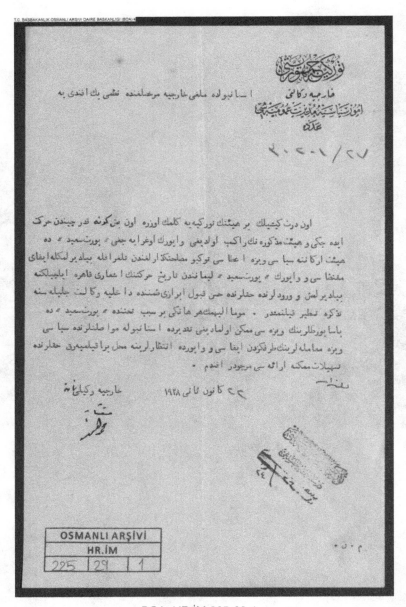

BCA, HR.İM 225-29-1
A delegation of 14 people will leave China to visit Turkey via Port Said.

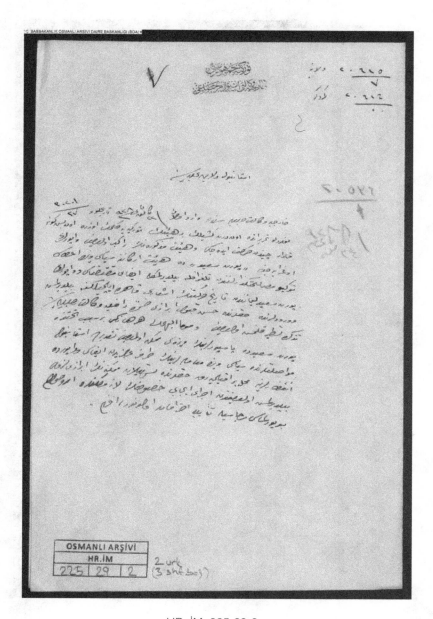

HR. İM. 225-29-2
A delegation of 14 people will leave China to visit Turkey via Port Said.
If it could not be possible to issue them a visa at Port Said, the visas should
be issued when they arrive İstanbul.

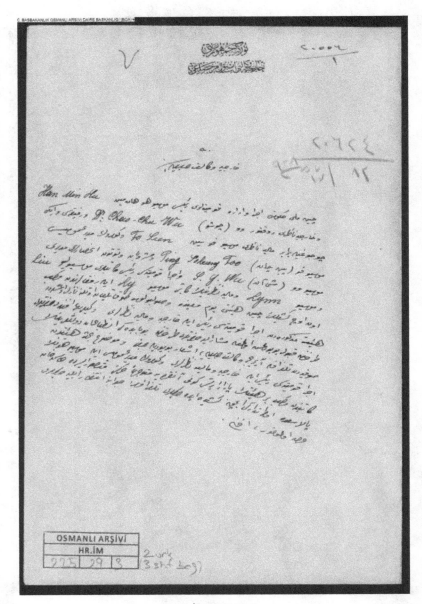

HR. İM 225-29-3
The delegation headed by Hu Hanmin, ministers and their family
arrived in the Tokatlıyan hotel in İstanbul.
The delegation will leave for Ankara on monday.

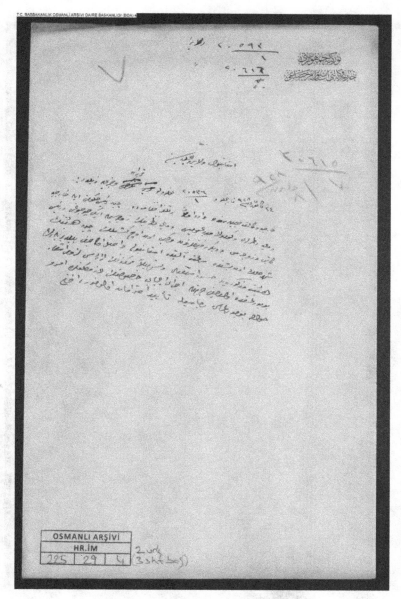

HR.İM-225-29-4
A delegation of the head of Chinese government and minister of
foreign affairs including other ministers and some of their family members
will arrive in İstanbul this month. A welcoming ceremony for their
arrival is required so inform the regarding departments.

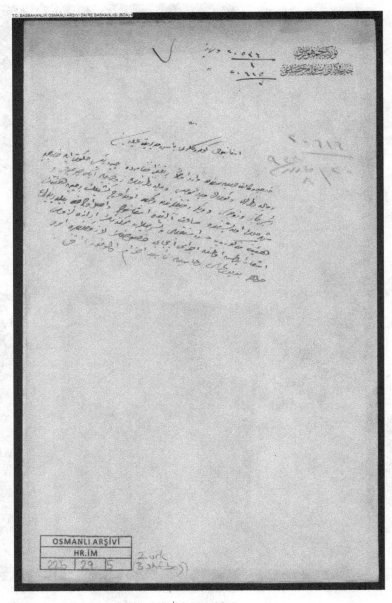

HR.İM-225-29-5
Please inform the regarding departments for the welcoming
ceremony of the Chinese delegation.

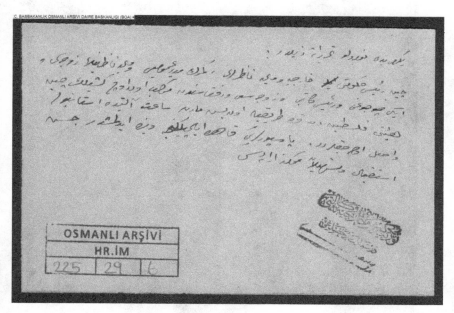

HR.İM-225-29-6
Chinese delegation will arrive by 15th of this month. Their passports
already issued visas by our embassy in Cairo.

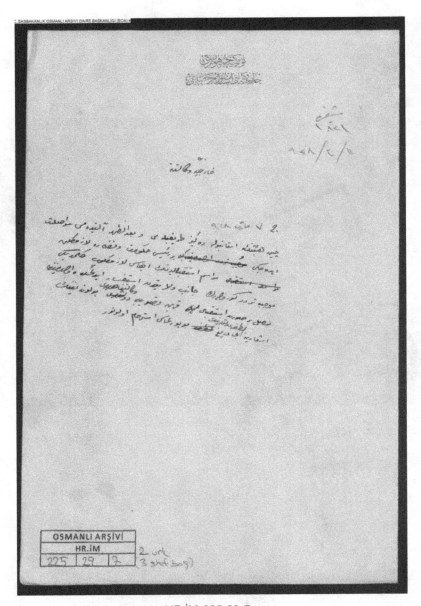

HR.İM-225-29-7
Asked if the head of Chinese Government and the delegation will arrive
in İstanbul by sea or land and the welcoming ceremony.

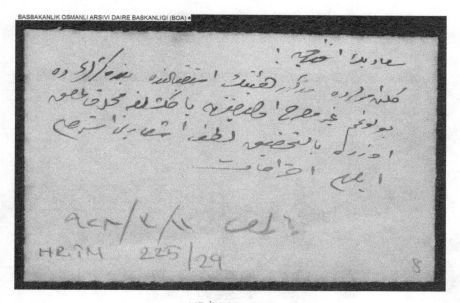

HR.İM-225-29-8

To Mr. Suad, it is not yet settled whether I will attend the welcoming ceremony so please make your preparations in advance for my absence. (Tevfik Rüştü Aras; minister of foreign affairs of the republic of Turkey between 1925-1939)

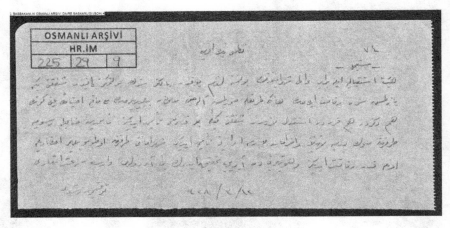

HR.İM-225-29-9
To Mr. Nazmi, there is no need the mayor to be in the welcoming ceremony.
Your presence will be enough. Arrange automobiles for the delegation
from the municipality. Please accompany the delegation until they arrive
the hotel and ask if they need anything. (Tevfik Rüştü Aras)

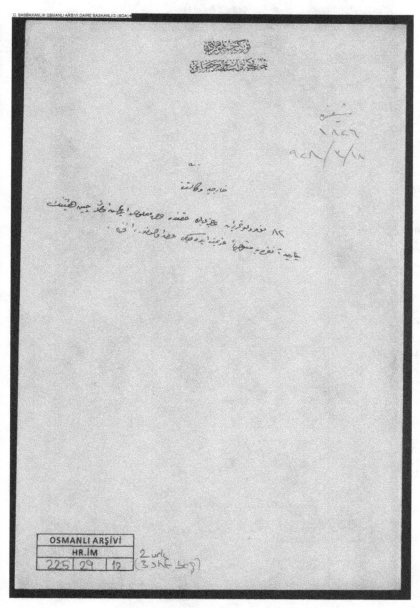

HR.İM-225-29-12
The Chinese delegation is heading towards Ankara today.

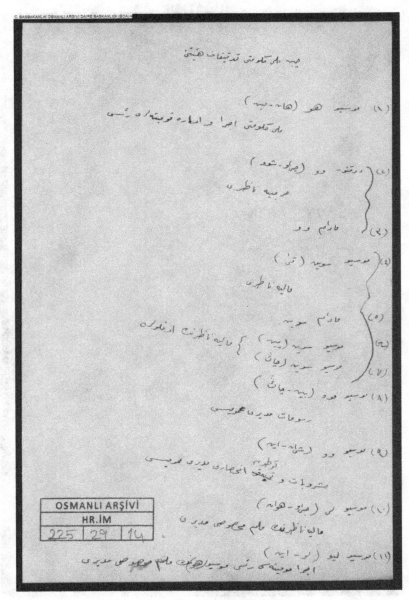

HR.İM-225-29-14
A list of the names of the Chinese Delegation written in Ottoman Turkish.

HR.İM-225-29-13
A list of the names of the Chinese Delegation written in Chinese and English.

nationalism on behalf of Islam? Can this kind of nationalism fully replace the belief of Islam?" The second point was: "Now Turkey has nationalism as its founding ideology. A new country has been established through nationalism, but it is not paying much attention to civil rights and people's livelihood. Isn't it necessary to make further progress in these fields in the future?" Regarding the first point, he answered: "We do not want Islamization because it is not enough for us to reach our goals." Some say: "The spirit of Islam is courageous. The spirit of Turkey's reviving nation-building has been greatly linked to Islam." In fact, this statement is not necessarily correct. Of all the previous wars that have been fought, the bravest and the most fiercely fighting soldiers were not Muslims but Non-Muslims.

All of his answers had a point. However, I thought that with the revival of Turkey, the spirit of Islam had its part. In ancient times, Muslims with a sword in one hand and a Quran in the other founded many countries based on this spirit. This spirit is in the Turks' blood, and this time was also one of them! Turkey's internal troubles, the era of suffering, later on became the brand new and the refined spirit of the country's recovery and rejuvenation. The Turks did not know how to achieve this amazing success. They thought that this was the spirit of nationalism, and they had forgotten the spirit of Islam. This is called "Do not know the true face of Lushan Mountain, but his body is in the mountain."[10] The Turks themselves did not understand themselves, but we outsiders clearly understood it at a glance.

Regarding the second point, he answered: "When we founded the country, we certainly needed to place extra emphasis on nationalism,

---

10. From a poem by Sushi (不知廬山眞面目，只緣身在此山中)

and only then could we establish a strong nation and country. Therefore, regarding civil rights and people's livelihood, we had some shortcomings. We need to gradually notice and solve these issues. As far as people's livelihood is concerned, there are very few workers in Turkey; in the machinery industry it can be said that there is not a single worker; farmers are the same way. Workers in the machine industry could say no, and farmers could do the same. Therefore, the Communist Party could not revolt. Now Turkey's solution to the issue of people's livelihoods is not about distribution but the creation of production. The economic aggression of the imperialists is most closely observed and elicits the most defensive policy from our new government. All foreigners who open a store in Turkey can hire foreigners as their managers. However, the subordinate managerial staff and workers must be Turks. Foreigners who do business in Turkey have to obey this ordinance. This method has created many jobs for Turks."

From this answer, we may know for sure that Turkey can quickly create a great and rejuvenated country because its intention is strongly spirited and is able to concentrate on nationalism. Sincerity splits and opens even the stone and the gold.[11] Turkey's success lies in this pure nationalist power. As for its flaws, it is biased towards nationalism and does not pay attention to civil rights and people's livelihood. Turkey has some shortcomings in civil rights, and its solution for people's livelihoods is to simply adopt a national economy and ban foreign businessmen from doing business. So, Turkey, after rejuvenating the country through nationalism, must work hard to

---

11. From Zhuangzi "精誠所注金石爲開."

solve the civil rights and the livelihood issues. By doing so, the politics of Turkey can reach perfection.

Second, I talked with one of Turkey's founding leaders.

Everyone knows Kemal. He is the first great character who created New Turkey. Talking about him is very interesting. In last two years, he has stopped caring about anything because he has been so sick and could not care about unpleasant matters. He is paying incognito visits, and the Turkish people adore him greatly. Everyone says: "He is the creator of New Turkey, the one, and the only benefactor. Let him have his leisure." It is tough to find Kemal; no one can easily meet him. When we were in the Turkish capital, we wanted to meet Kemal, but did not know where he was. It can be said that it was İsmet Pasha who took power in the name of and ruled on behalf of Kemal. He was a man of military origin: courageous and diligent. I met İsmet Pasha and had an in-depth conversation with him. This man is truly eye-catching and glorious and has a glorious gaze of a leader that founded a nation. He was the chief representative to the Lausanne Congress. At the conference in Lausanne, he was a very fierce player and caused many European delegates to be amazed by this strange figure. When I met him, I said: "You were really successful at the Lausanne Conference."

"You flatter me; this is not a success. We were the victorious country. Of course, we must get this result." He was dignified and, at the very same time, coldly asked me "Were you diplomatically unsuccessful?"

"This is not necessarily the case. This is not our diplomatic success. It is the success of the strength of our national unity. At that time all our nation from top to bottom was as one and willing to struggle. If we could not be successful at the Lausanne Conference, we would immediately have withdrawn from the conference and declared war! So, this cannot be considered our diplomatic success." His answers were all very reasonable. It can be seen that their success at that time was not accidental. Later, when we talked about the general relationship between the party and the government, I asked: "What is the relationship between your party and the government?"

"When it comes to the relationship between our party and the government, I can take a very obvious fact to inform: Kemal is our president. At the same time, he is the leader of our party; I am the Prime Minister of the Cabinet. At the same time, I represent Kemal, and I also represent Kemal as the party's prime minister." He was very straightforward; this response demonstrated the spirit of İsmet Pasha and the spirit of the new Turkish politics. We continued and also talked about the questions surrounding the system of committees. When I asked about the advantages and disadvantages of this system and the situation of the Turkish government regarding the aforementioned system, he honestly stated: "I do not believe that the system of committees can have a great deal of success. Under a wise and capable leadership, it will be successful and effective. The committee system must be much more than that. In the future, in the political organizations, the effectiveness of this system will be minimal!"

Later, he also asked us about the relations between the doctrine of the Chinese Revolution, the party, and government and I told him the situation. I also asked him: "Can Turkey be like China in the future?"[12]

---

12. Referring to the political system in China.

He said: "This is a different situation in different countries. China has its unique circumstances. Take Turkey in a comparison to China; we are only equivalent to one province of China. So, we cannot do this according to China." His few words were, indeed, very accurate. These were my meetings with the members of the new government of Turkey.

Third, the characteristics of the new Turkish government.

On characteristics of the new Turkish government, we can see a few points. The first is it must work hard to disseminate education. The general level of knowledge of the Turkish people is very shameful. The new government must create new businesses and must disseminate knowledge in order to do that. For instance, the Turkish government ordered foreign businesses to employ Turks, allowing that managers could be foreigners. Foreign investors obey the Turkish government's decree, but the Turks' level of knowledge has not been sufficient for business. This has been a flaw. Therefore, in this regard, it is not a question of rights, but a question of capability. The new government has, therefore, established a large-scale teacher education program, and teacher education is the first step in disseminating education nationwide. We believe that the new government of Turkey will certainly have great achievements in education.

The second step is the fiscal unification. The most expressive new spirit in Turkey's politics is the orderliness of finances without any private mischief. Other countries' financial habits cannot be found in Turkey. During the war, the army retreated to Ankara, and Kemal ordered the finances of the military to be united under the land forces. Later on, all budgets were united under the land forces'. He believed this was not enough and ordered all the budgets to be united under the ministry of finance. Kemal's uniting of finances and his perseverance is admirable. The new politics' success and failure are directly related to the unification of the fiscal system!

The fourth is that the unity of command can be considered a special spirit of the new government of Turkey. Kemal, when creating new policies, pays attention to this point. He had ordered that all the red hats (fez) worn by the Turkish people be taken off within twenty-four hours. As a result, all people of Turkey did not hesitate to take off the red hats. We need to hold a new political agenda that guarantees the obedience to the orders of the government by the entire nation immediately. Otherwise, the government's practices make no sense, and the orders of the government would have no effect. I want to ask how such a government can implement its politics. The revival of Turkey is not accidental. We, with our comrades carrying out the Three Principles of the People and our eyes on the Turkish progress, which advances at a tremendous pace, will be successful for sure.

Reflections of Hu Hanmin's visit to Turkey in Turkish Newspapers

"The Chinese Government Came to Our City Yesterday" [xxii]

There is only one man in National China who is appreciated, even worshipped: Gazi Mustafa Kemal! This is the statement of the Chinese delegation and the Minister of Foreign Affairs.

The national Chinese government delegation arrived at Haidar Pasha station yesterday. The head of the Central Committee of the Chinese government, Monsieur (Huhamin), Monsieur (Shav-Shu-

"Çin Hükümeti Dün Şehrimize Geldi," Milliyet, March 16, 1928.

"Çin Hükümeti Dün Şehrimize Geldi," Milliyet, March 16, 1928.

Vu), the minister of foreign affairs, and Monsieur (Osum), the minister of finance, along with a delegation came to our city yesterday evening by a train from Syria. Within the delegation, there are customs officers, wives of the ministers of foreign affairs and finance, and their children. The Chinese national delegation, consisting of thirteen people, female and male, was warmly welcomed at the Haidar Pasha station yesterday evening.

The Chinese students in our city welcomed the National Government of Nanjing. The students, who bear the national flags of Turkey and China, greeted the delegation as soon as the train arrived by shouting "Hurrah, Long Live!" The students were also holding banners in their hands written in both Turkish and Chinese: "Long live Turkey, Long live the National Government of China!" The delegation was welcomed by Nazmi Bey on behalf of the foreign affairs ministry. On behalf of the municipality [deputy mayor] Hamid, the police, and constabulary performed the official salutation.

From this sincere welcome, the Chinese national government officials were very happy, were taken to dock at Galata, got on the İstanbul boat assigned for them and went to the Tokatlıyan Hotel.

The Chinese patriots, dressed fully in Western style clothing, spoke Chinese and English. One of our reporters interviewed the Chinese patriots. The delegation repeatedly stated their happiness to come to Turkey and showed great interest towards İstanbul. The women in the delegation were especially eager to learn more about the Bosphorus. In this regard, the elegant minister of foreign affairs cheerfully asked about the Yıldız Palace. The minister of foreign affairs of China, Monsieur (Shav-Shu-Vu), who talked for a long time with our reporter, has given the following information about their travel:

We have been traveling for two months now. We went to Egypt, Palestine, and Syria. In these countries, we have been very generously welcomed.

The Chinese foreign minister mostly answered our reporter's questions regarding China very briefly and asked: "Is this the Bosphorus? Is this the Golden Horn?" By asking such questions, he tried to get information about Istanbul from our reporter. Finally, after our reporter insisted on asking questions about China, the minister of foreign affairs replied by talking about the national flag of China, which was now raised in the hands of the Chinese students.

The National Flag of China

Our flag, which consists of a sun on a blue background, is a symbol that shows how much we love our country and independence. We want to be as clear as the sky, and as bright as the sun.

Meanwhile the boat was passing by Sarayburnu. When he saw the statue of the Gazi (Mustafa Kemal), he immediately took off his hat and bowed down twice saying "Gazi, Gazi."

Monsieur (Şav-Şu-Vu) continued to talk about China and said: "Today, true China consists of twenty-eight provinces. Sixteen of these are entirely in the hands of the Chinese national government. But Manchuria, Tibet, and Turkistan are not among these provinces."

Hair being cut

Almost everybody within the national government areas has cut their hair. But this is not an obligation. The ones who wish to have long hair can have their hair long. However, day by day, more and more people are seen without long hair.

Within the areas controlled by the Chinese National government, just as during the old Ottoman government times, there are still capitulations and unfair custom tariffs and so on.

We envy Turkey

The foreign minister replied to our reporter about his feelings regarding Turkey as follows: "My feelings regarding Turkey are so great that I do not think I can explain them briefly. Turkey is very well-known within the borders of Nationalist China. Turkey's revolutions were met with admiration and envy in Nationalist China. You are now a totally free and independent nation that got rid of the capitulations, and you owe this to your great guide, Gazi. Mustafa Kemal's name is respected everywhere in China. You are fortunate: Turkey is free and independent. We, the Chinese patriots, are also working to create a free and independent China. This is our politics within and outside of our country." The Chinese foreign minister told us that the delegation will stay in İstanbul and observe our revolutions and then leave for Ankara and that the delegation is grateful for the hospitality.

"The Chinese Delegation Came to Our City Yesterday"[xxiii]

The delegation of the national Nanjing government is observing our civilized country. The head of the Chinese foreign affairs committee told our reporter: "The delegation consists of the ministers of the

Nanjing government and is on a survey trip to Europe and America."
The Chinese delegation arrived in our city yesterday. The Chinese
delegation was welcomed by the official from the ministry of foreign
affairs Sefketi Bey, deputy governor, deputy mayor, and the director
of the fifth branch of the police in Haidar Pasha train station. At the
welcoming ceremony, a police squadron greeted the delegation and
Chinese students in our city were also present. Chinese students were
holding Turkish and Nanjing government flags in their hands. Furthermore, students held banners written in Turkish and Chinese:
"Long live the Republic of Turkey," "Long live the Republic of
China," and "Warmly Welcoming You." The delegation, amidst the
applause of the students, got on a boat and went to the Tokatlıyan
Hotel.

The Chinese delegation consists of the chairman of the government executive committee, Monsieur (Hu-Han-Min), and the finance
minister, monsieur (Sun-Ti-Ni). The customs director of the Nanjing
government and their wives and children accompany the delegation.
A group of thirteen people, the Chinese guests are traveling in a private train car.

The foreign minister of the Nanjing government, Monsieur (Şai-
Şu-Vu), told our reporter: "We left China around two months ago.
We have visited Egypt, Palestine, Syria, and are now visiting Turkey.
Our goal is surveying the political and economic developments in
Europe and America for the development of our country. After staying for 10 days in İstanbul, we will then go to Ankara. Later on, we
will visit all of the Europe and America and finally return to our
country. As you know, we rebelled against the government of Peking
and established a national and patriotic government. The most im-

"Çin Heyeti Dün şehrimize Geldi," Vakit Newspaper, March 16, 1928.

portant part of the Chinese empire is the Original China.[13] Sixteen of these provinces of China are now under the control of the Nanjing government. So, most of the Chinese people are now participating in the national movement and national government. Manchuria, Tibet, and Turkistan are detached for now."

Our present-day situation is exactly the same as Turkey's in the armistice days. In our case, the Peking government represents the İstanbul government, and the Nanjing government represents the Ankara government. We, the people of Nanjing, are determined to rescue China from foreign oppression.

This can be achieved in two words: independence and legitimacy. In this regard, in recent years, we have closely watched Turkey's victory against the foreign oppression. Turkey is our model in our struggle for independence. It is our greatest desire to visit Gazi. Therefore, we wanted to visit Turkey and Ankara in the first phase of our journey.

The Nanjing government is governed by a central executive committee which consists of forty members. We do not have a prime minister (the head of the government). The head of our executive committee is Monsieur (Ha-Han-Min), who is traveling with our delegation. In Nanjing, the foreign capitulations are still in force. But we will soon save China from this disgrace. We in Nanjing have a totally patriotic and pro-Turkish government. Now our citizens do not have their hair long. Our women participate in public life. In a nutshell, the nationalist government of China is progressing in every aspect.

---

13. He must be referring to China Proper.

"The National Delegation of China Comes to Our City"[xxiv]

The minister of foreign affairs says that the Chinese patriots are closely observing Turkey.

The delegation traveling on behalf of the Chinese "National Nanjing" government came to our city by train from Palestine.

The delegation was welcomed in Haidar Pasha train station by the deputy governor, Tahsin Bey, the deputy mayor, Hamid Bey, a foreign affairs official, Şefkati Bey, and Kenan Bey, the director of the fifth branch of the police.

Meanwhile a platoon of police and constabulary performed a welcome ceremony. The Chinese merchants and students in our city welcomed the delegation holding Turkish and Nanjing government flags and banners written in both Turkish and Chinese: "Long live the Nationalist Republic of China" and "Long live the Republic of Turkey."

The delegation consisted of three people: the head of the National Nanjing executing committee, monsieur Hu Hanmin; the minister of foreign affairs, monsieur "şuşavu"; and the minister of finance monsieur, "Sonki," and their wives and children.

The delegation went to the Tokatlıyan Hotel with the municipality's boats. One of our reporters spoke to the minister of foreign affairs, monsiuer "Şuşavu". He said:

"We left Nanjing two months ago. We went to Egypt and Palestine. And now, we are here in Turkey. We will stay for 10 days here. During this period, we will go to Ankara and see his excellency Gazi. After Turkey we will tour all of the Europe and America."

— "Could you please explain the purpose of your trip?"

"Milli Çin Heyeti Şehrimize Geldi," Cumhuriyet Newspaper, March 16, 1928.

— "Our purpose is to observe the political and commercial situation. As you know, there are two governments in China now. One is national; the other is conservative. It is just like how you once had the İstanbul and Ankara governments. We are traveling on behalf of the "National Nanjing" government. And sixteen of the twenty-eight provinces of China are subject to us. The other twelve provinces, including Manchuria, Tibet, and Turkestan, are loyal to the conservative Peking government."

— "What is your government's goal?"

— "I can summarize it with two words: independence and legitimacy. We closely observe Turkey. Our newspapers reported the Turkish victory and struggle for independence. China's situation now is exactly the same as that of old Turkey. Unfortunately, we still cannot get rid of the capitulations."

— "Who is your prime minister?"

— "We are governed by a committee of thirty to forty people. The government does not have a prime minister."

— "How did you find Istanbul?"

— "I have not seen anything yet (looking toward Bosphorus). It is probably very beautiful."

It is probable that the Chinese delegation will be accepted by Tevfik Rüşdü Bey, the minister of foreign affairs.

CHAPTER 3

Ankara: The New Capital of Turkey[xxv]

Unfortunately, there is no information available on the author Wang Huishan in Chinese sources. Only this short travelogue has survived.

Ankara was a small town in Asia Minor with no significant place in history. In 1919, after the breakout of the Greco-Turkish war, the Turkish Nationalist Party with Mustafa Kemal as its leader gathered troops and resisted the Greeks. Later, they defeated the Greek Army. Turkish territory formerly occupied by foreign powers was entirely returned to the Turks, and they pushed the Greek Army outside of its borders to the west. At this time, the Young Turk Party established their political center in Ankara against the sultan's government in İstanbul. Due to the results of the steady military victory of the party, Ankara became an important point at home and abroad. In 1921, the Kuomintang [i.e., the Turkish Nationalist Party] won a complete victory and overthrew the sultan, and the thus ended the Ottoman Empire. The party's army established the government in Ankara, and after the fulfillment of independence and the Lausanne treaty, all was in a stable situation. On October 29, 1923, the state system was announced as a republic. At this time, the Turkish army had already defeated the Greek army, and the troops of various countries that occupied Constantinople have also gradually retreated. Yet, the Great

Power's influence has not been completely eradicated. Constantinople is a coastal city. If something happens, European ships can arrive very quickly and can threaten the capital city. Ankara, on the other hand, is very far from the sea, and therefore it is not an easy target to shell. Most of the Turkish territory in Europe has been lost, but only Edirne and Constantinople remained at that time. Turkey's center was Constantinople, so the nationalist government thought that it should run its government in Asia Minor. As a result of these two reasons, it decided to abandon the old capital city of Constantinople and choose Ankara as the capital of the Republic of Turkey. Consequently, Ankara, this small city, became the center of Turkey's government. This became the place for foreign reporters and politicians to visit. After 1922 Turkey toppled down the last of the Ottoman emperors who had already lived for generations in the Roman city. Turkey's first capital city was Konya (Konia) in Asia Minor. It was a former Roman city. Later on, the capital moved to Bursa and Edirne (Adrine or Adrianople). Finally, the capital city was Constantinople, which had been established as the capital city of the Eastern Roman Empire. Moreover, the Republic of Turkey was founded. The central government and the capital city moved to the east to a purely Turkish-style town. Ankara in ancient times had been occupied by Persians and Arabs. In Roman times, there were too many of the famous temples to the east in the city. As the years went by, they were all obliterated. Moreover, the Seljuks (Seljuq or Seljucide, the ancestors of the Turks) after conquering the territories, manufactured weapons to defeat the enemy. These Turks still remain today. Later, Timur leading the Mongolians attacked to the west, including Ankara. In 1833, King Ali of Egypt, a separatist landlord, seized Ankara.

However, soon afterward, the territories returned to the Turks. The next invasion was in 1922 by Trikoupis [at the head of the Greek army], who advanced deeply into Turkey and reached a place 90 kilometers away from Ankara. He was defeated by the National Revolutionary forces of Turkey. In 1918 there was a big fire in Ankara, and the city completely turned into ashes. The capital city of a country is the political hub of the country. The views of all parties must not be random; this is something everyone knows. However, Turkey's capital city—Ankara—is not like this. The narrow streets and old buildings make one not to dare to think of it is a country's capital city at first sight. Ankara is now roughly divided into two parts: One is called the New City, and the other is the Old City. The Old City refers to the old Ankara on the mountainside. The roads are constructed with square and small circle gravel of different sizes, all uneven, with many twists and turns. Although there are one or two slightly better trails upon which to drive cars, in the middle of the journey, if you come across a vehicle you would have great difficulties. If you do not drive your car into the yard of a house, the car coming from the opposite direction cannot drive further. This is how narrow the roads are. Houses are mostly old Turkish-style, with small windows and round domes with stone walls that all are uneven. Eighty percent of the residents are local natives. There is no difference in the customary clothing with the other parts of Asia Minor and the small Asian minorities. Chants coming from a small ancient mosque calling people to prayer are heard on every street. Standing the the heights of the old city and looking to the west, one can see several streets and buildings called the "New City." Now the capital city of Turkey is in this new city. The new city is certainly much better than the old one. The area is flat, and the roads are made of small blocks of ashlar. Although not very wide, vehicles can just pass through in two directions. Except for the horse manure and mud, the streets are clean. There are four main streets, and two streets lead to the commercial district. One street is called as the Balık Pazarı [Fish Bazaar], while the other is called as the Taşhan Caddesi (Taşhan Street). These two streets intersect each other, and all of Ankara's stores are located on these two streets. The remaining two streets are called Cumhuriyet Caddesi (Republic Street) and Meclis Caddesi (The National Assembly Street). Cumhuriyet Caddesi is newly constructed. It is the newest and the best street in Ankara and leads directly to the railway station.

The organization of the Turkish government, for a Chinese citizen like me, seems very simple. Excepting the government, ministry buildings, and parliament, there is only a police station, a gendarmerie post, an aviation department, a postal service bureau, and the Nationalist Party headquarters. Besides these, there is no other institution in sight. All these buildings, more than ten in number, are constructed in a line on Cumhuriyet Caddesi and are situated across the road from each other. If a person wants to go from one institution to another, he does not need to find a car or horse carriage but just needs to walk a few steps. The State Council is across from the Police Department. If the prime minister wants to see the police chief, he does not need to call him by phone but only open the window and wave his hand. The Ministry of Finance and the State Council are located in the same building. The State Council is upstairs, and the Ministry of Finance is downstairs. The offices of the Ankara government are simple in appearance, and the interior of the building is also similar.

For each ministry, there is a plate hung next to the door with the name of the ministry written on it. The inside of the ministry is, of course, divided into offices. Within the ministry, the minister and all departments also have plates written on them hung on the doors. It is written clearly, "the office of the minister" or certain department. Anyone can enter the offices freely; this saves time and simplifies formalities. Upon entering the office of a department, there is a single window inside, a bookcase, and a few armchairs. On the bookcase there is ink and other stationery, and some offices have telephones. The head of the department, every day, at a certain time (in the morning from 9 to 12, and in the afternoon from 2 to 5) sits in this small room, holds a pen in the right hand, the telephone headset in the left hand, and his eyes on official documents, and works all day. He also has an assistant at his side (also called a staff member). This is the form of ministries and departments of the Republic of Turkey. The presidential palace and residence are a little further away. Past a hillside in the northwest of the new city, the place is called Çankaya. The place is in quite good shape. Residences of the other important people are also located in this neighborhood. The Parliament building is behind the State Council building. Although the scale is not very large the building is neat and solemn. Entering from the gate, there is the main hall. The interior is arranged as a small theater with seats for 300 members. There are additional seats for guests. There is a plaque hanging on the front of the main hall: "sovereignty belongs to the people." Apart from primary schools, there are both male and female secondary schools and normal schools; there is also a law school. It is a branch of Istanbul University in Constantinople and was newly established in 1926. Among the primary schools, the latest and the most complete one is the Gazi Primary School established by the Great General President Kemal. Ankara's only newspaper is called *Hakimiyet-i Milliye*, and now it releases an evening paper. It started publishing on the New Year's day in 1927. It can be said that there is not a single hotel in Ankara; there is only one second-class guest house called Taşhan. It is poorly equipped and not clean. When foreign envoys and guests come to Ankara, there was nowhere to stay, so a businessman with government funding, constructed on the opposite side of the parliament a new and large-scale hotel called Ankara Palace. It was opened in January 1927. Other buildings such as theaters are few. For local residents, besides tea and coffee houses, there is only a dance hall in a remote place and a small cinema hall constructed last year. Although Ankara is the new capital city, the embassies of many countries are still in Constantinople. In case of an important incident in ordinary times, an envoy comes temporarily to Ankara and then returns to Istanbul. For now, there is no place for the officials of various countries to live, and the Turkish government is also unable to provide for them. It ordered several trains to be prepared in the train station so foreign ambassadors and officials can use them as their offices. Now many of them are purchasing land for constructing their embassies, and they will gradually move here. Due to its remote location, Ankara cannot produce anything, and also there is no industry to talk about. All of the shops in the town sell goods coming from İstanbul. The cost of living here is very high, at least three times higher than İstanbul. Although trams have been planned for a long time, they have not been built yet. The transportation in the city is dependent on automobiles, but there is only one road from Republic Road to the railway station. There are old-fashioned bull carts for the transport of goods, and there are trains for the long-distance traffic. Westward, İstanbul can be reached in 20 hours by railway; it goes to Berlin from the Balkans and then to the south-east from Asia Minor. According to the census of 1837, there were 28,000 people living here (Ankara). In 1865 there were 25,000 Turks, 12,000 Catholic Armenians, 3,000 Greeks, and around 1,000 Jews. After the fire, more than half of the Armenians and Greeks fled, and the total population was only 35,000. According to 1923 census, after the war around 90,000 persons went to Greece and Armenia. The population has been greatly reduced. According to the recent survey in January 1927, there are 35,000 Turks, and no more than 6,000 for-eigners. There are about 6.000 households. The climate is not very cold or very hot. The rainfall is quite heavy. In winter, it is windy, and, when the wind blows, dust flies around. After rain, everywhere is muddy and it is difficult to walk. It is quite annoying. Historical monuments are in the old part of the city. At its highest point there is a small castle dating back 1,000 years. There is a very famous mosque close to the new city called Hacı Bayram. It was constructed over an old Roman temple. Behind this mosque, there is a Roman temple. The Turks call it the Augustus Temple. It is in ruins now, but there are still half of the stone tablets engraved in Latin. There is a stone pillar close to the State Council building called Kız Taşı [Girl Stone]. It is also a Roman relic. Ankara was a village and suddenly became the capital city. The Turkish government is making plans for all kinds of construction; for instance the building of the tramway, the construction of roads, the establishment of water and electric companies, and the construction of housing projects are all underway. In the future Ankara will gradually break away from this rudimentary situation and will have a great view. Now the people of Ankara are commemorating the great achievements of great president Kemal. At the crossroads of the new Republic Street, they are building a bronze statue of him. It will take 6 months to build it. To sum up, the new capital city of Turkey, Ankara, is from the outside rusty and unbearably crude, but its substance is neat and strong. Only three years after the establishment of the Republic of Turkey, looking at the reforms and progress in all aspects of internal affairs and diplomacy accomplished in such a short period of time will cause everyone to envy beyond imagination: Turkey's powerful Republican Party government issuing orders and devising strategies from this rusty and crude Ankara! It can clearly be seen that the safety and prosperity of a country does not depend on the gorgeousness of the capital city. It depends on the unity of the nation from top to bottom and steady and strong government!

CHAPTER 4

He Yaozu on Turkey

He Yaozu was born in 1889. He was a general and the first ambassador appointed to Turkey. While he was in Turkey between 1934 and 1937, he wrote extensively on Turkey's modernization and nation-building process.

Nation-Building of Turkey and
Three Principles of the People[xxvi]

I was enlisted to be the ambassador to Turkey, and before heading to Turkey, the newspapers gave me a lot of instructions and encouragements. I was hoping that I would study the issues of Turkey and find ways of handling matters for our country. The newspapers wanted me to study these following three points:

1. Turkey as a country between Fascism and Communism. The country was neutral and created its own cultural center.

2. Turkish politics is similar to autocracy and one-party dictatorship, but the parliament still exists and is able to continue its activities. How can this happen?

3. The economic development of Turkey started not long ago. How could they achieve economic recovery and improve the living standard of the general public?

All newspapers published all these questions until I left the country. On all occasions, they told me their hope of understanding these matters. Now, after returning home and having studied the matters there profoundly, I will answer these questions.

1. Turkey is a country between Fascism and Communism. The country was neutral and created its own cultural center. I think that the establishment of the modern state, in addition to domestic and foreign affairs and economic development, had two very important factors that cannot be ignored. One is the national idea, and the other one is the culture. If a country has a profound national idea, and at the same time a high degree of cultural level of the nation, then foreign forces and ideas cannot invade, and vice versa. If the national idea is not strong enough and lacks a cultural center, the nation will be like a hungry person. Regarding the food, there is no choice but to eat anything. As a result, not only is there ideological and cultural invasion, but the entire nation will face a serious problem of survival. The Premier [Sun Yatsen], in his speech on nationalism, advocated our native culture, mentioned the modern national survival struggle, and urged us to be vigilant about the issue. This was a great lesson and showed foresight that we should never forget. Turkey has been able to eliminate foreign aggression and resist the intrusion of foreign ideas because they have a profound national idea and universally teach their culture. This historical fact was not created overnight. The most obvious two examples were to move the capital city and the population exchange with other countries. The reason for moving the capital, although it is clearly understood from the defense issue, is undeniable in that this decision would arouse national consciousness, national ideology, and national feelings. According to the history of

Turkey, the birthplace of the Turkish nation is Anatolia, and returning to Ankara is no different than returning to the birthplace of the nation. The people of Turkey were also convinced that this move is of great benefit to the nation and endorsed by everyone. About the issue of population exchange, according to the Lausanne Treaty of January 1922, all ethnic minorities based on nationality or religion can be easily exchanged. Thus as with the Turkish Greeks. There were 1.35 million people who moved out of the Turkish borders, and between 1921 and 1927 432,000 Turks moved into Turkey. After this [population exchange] with Greece, the two countries signed a mutual agreement, and people moved around more conveniently. Many Turks fled into Turkey, abandoned their properties in Bulgaria and Greece, and came back to their country. This meant that they never accept to be ruled by another nation, and the national culture has never been lost. This is a profound kind of nationalism! I am afraid that people in China cannot even dream of such a thing. Other Balkan peoples, although under the rule of the Ottoman Empire through hundreds of years, always had a deep hatred for each other. Soldiers from both sides meet each other frequently and there was no possibility of assimilating to each other. It can be seen that the nationalistic ideas of the peoples in this area are very strong. It is no accident that the Turks abandoned the false ideals of the great empire and Pan-Islamism and entered the path of nationalism.

Turkey has such a strong and deep nationalism. Therefore, the Communist red tide will calm down as soon as it reaches the border of Turkey. This is not surprising. The Russian and Turkish alliance can be said to exist only for the purpose of securing Russia's southern gates, and Russia does not have the ambition to interfere in Turkey's internal affairs. Russia's help to Turkey in the Montreux Convention is for the national defense of the straits and nothing more than this. As far as fascism is concerned, the expression of extreme nationalism is nothing but a product of the social, political, economic, and national nature of a certain nation. It is not static thus it contains internationality. The Turkish revolution succeeds in bringing about vitality. Successes after great defeats, the old and the new thoughts and conflicts were overwhelming, and they could not be handled without a parliament. Using constitutionalism to express the spirit of democracy is bound to hinder the unity of the nation and to decisively open the parliament to implement fascism. This is something Kemal does not like. Looking at Turkey, in the middle of communism and fascism, it can stand on its own. In simple words, because nationalism and Islamic culture are enriched within, the spiritual life of the people is self-sufficient. The Premier[14] said: "Nationalism is for all people living in the country," and also said that "China has nepotism and clannism but does not have nationalism." We see the successful example of Turkey, and we see the grave threat to the survival of the nation. Can we not think about it?

2. Turkish politics is similar to autocracy and one-party dictatorship, but the parliament still exists and is able to continue its activities. How can this happen? Based on the Premier's idea of democracy, we will found a national assembly; formulate the constitution and so on. It is all very similar to the Turkish government's political guidance. However, when the Premier talks about nationalism before the implementation of constitutional government in

---

14. Refers to Sun Yatsen

Ambassador He Yaozu in 1935 while on his way to Turkish Presidency
to offer his letter of credence.[xxvii]

Turkey, we were about to implement a constitutional government. After Turkey's effective and successful implementation of constitution, it became a model for us. I think there are so many similarities between our two countries, and it is all because of the necessities of their environment. If we look at the generation and implementation of the Turkish constitution, we can understand the embryonic development and growth of the modern Turkish state and politics. It is due to the revolutionary trend of thought, national culture, economic affairs, and the international environment. Turkey's military affairs had ended, but not yet the implementation of the constitution. The people still questioned how the country's political bodies were to be settled; that is, the Republican People's Party was not established yet. There were Republicans, Restorationists,[15] and localist factions in parliament. They all had their own newspapers, and their attacks on the cabinet members were quite intense. They further collaborated with the conservatives and the caliph and advocated that the staff of the party and the government organs should be distributed equally among the provincial and district representatives according to their numbers. Although they have no noble purpose and ideal, they are inspired by their aims. They were large in number in the parliament; thus Kemal organized a committee to elect the ministers. And so, private residences and public places were full of them discussing how to form a cabinet. But with further discussion, the more miscellaneous the ideas became, and the more the spirit had to struggle with many hours of debate. A majority could not be reached for the passing of the cabinet. At this time, Kemal already knew the shortcom-

---

15. Conservatives

ings of the temporary law. Think of the method of organizing the government: you must find a way to implement what you said at the time. You can think of it as Kemal says: "I think that the council's committee cannot achieve the decision of the cabinet's hope, I must be responsible for proposing after negotiations, and the time will pass, and the republic must be announced tomorrow. According to the current situation, we should cancel the doctrine of majority decision. I have decided to shorten procedures, starting from today, and decisions will be implemented immediately. The instructions for the gentlemen are that the state is a republic, and there will be no more discussions." This statement of Kemal, needless to say, was based upon his experience. All these fractions coincidentally achieved some successes. Lacking administrative effectiveness at the same time, it was hard to avoid being weak. This could cause disputes and unintentional sacrifices. For the well-being of the country, Kemal Pasha and İsmet Pasha discussed the provisional law of January 1, 1921, and added to Article One the phrase "The Turkish State is a republic," and to Article Three "All administrative ministers intend to direct the National Assembly and are responsible for guiding its management." Second, as to how the government is organized and how the president and premier are elected, there are explicit provisions. However, when the parliament meets, it is still like the turmoil of the past: the discussions on the formation of the cabinet, the public opinions, and the essentials. Therefore, some members proposed that Kemal be the "unique opinion maker" in order to break the deadlock, and the draft constitution was adopted after revisions and discussions that lasted 4 and a half hours.

At the closing ceremony of the parliament at 6 p.m. on October 29, 1923, Kemal declared the new constitution and made a four-point statement:

1. Sovereignty definitely belongs to the people, and the mode of government is actually established on the principle of the people's government.

2. For the sake of clarity and certainty: we declare the abolition of the monarchy and establish a republic, and the election of a president is underway.

3. For the sake of accountability, the Prime Minister should be appointed by the President. In this sense, a country, especially a country with a critical national defense situation, with its many industries languishing, a low level of cultural standards, and a disorderly social order, wants to establish the national defense, build culture, control the economy, and stabilize society. What kind of political system should be established?

The points made by Kemal have listed the constitution and, in particular, one part of the constitution. As far as the power of parliament is concerned, there is scope for activity in the constitutional legislative power. We do not infringe upon this kind of legislative power. The power of the three-power system is, of course, irreproachable. Therefore, the theory that the people of my country should believe in the power of the prime minister and the draft constitution decided by the party is a combination of our current needs and the international environment. The success of the Turkish constitutional system can greatly enhance our confidence.

4. The economic development of Turkey started not long ago. How could they achieve the economic recovery and improve the living

standards of the general public? The construction of the economy, the self-confidence of the nation, and the improvement of the economy and culture are inseparable. The economy of a nation being degraded and the culture being raised at the same time is impossible. Guan Zi[16] says, "Courtesy and justice, among the four dimensions of the country" but at the same time says: "when the people have enough food and clothing, they will know what is honor." Here we can see the relationship between economics and morality. On one hand, the premier advocates the restoration of the national morality. On the other hand, he also states that "the foundation of nation-building is the people's livelihood." After President Chiang Kai-shek advocated a new life movement, he followed the national economic construction movement. This is the faithful executor of the Premier [Sun Yatsen]'s legacy. After Turkey dealt with its external problems and established a constitutional government, it began to develop its economy. If we want to understand that the new stage of economic construction in Turkey, we first need to understand the revolution, the national economy, and finance and commercial issues resulting from most of the power being in the hand of the foreigners. Turkey used agriculture to build the country. The peasants constitute 80 percent of the total population. However, the state of agriculture is far below that of our country. The peasants are all accustomed to low-level life, and it is the same with our current situation. After the revolution, the government of Turkey focused on organizing finances: stabilizing the currency system, managing exchanges, restricting input, rewarding sales, promoting industry, improving agriculture,

16. Guan Zhong or Guan Zi, a Chinese philosopher and politician lived between 720 and 645 BCE.

developing transportation, promoting the aviation industry, and re-
pairing railways, docks, running water, and railways, and telephones,
etc. The establishment of a national economy, to the present day, has
always been consistent. At the beginning of the discussions, there
was a debate on being an industrial or an agricultural country. As a
result, the government decided upon a policy to attach equal importance to agriculture and industry, to improve agriculture, and then to
develop light industry according to the requirements of the peasants'
lives. Heavy industry also contributed to the development of agriculture. Seeds, fertilizers, new agricultural tools and methods have
improved the rural economy, and financial resources have been provided to farmers from several cooperatives and banks. The commer-
cialization of agricultural products has been actively pursued. Thus,
the harvest has increased by 20 million pounds; 3% annual interest
and 15-year repayment loans to farmers have been provided. The
government has also distributed free seeds worth 2 million pounds
to poor farmers. Agricultural products are not only raw materials but
also an important export item and have substantially contributed to
the import-export balance. This, in particular, has been one of the issues that the government has been paying attention to since 1929.

Second, Turkey, with regards to the development of its industry,
is aware of the fact that under the oppression of the European powers,
extraordinary means must be taken to support its own industry. It has
decided to adopt a national control policy and seek independence for
its own economy. The primary objective is to increase the number
of products produced by the national industry. Determined to limit
foreign intrusion and to secure the development of the industry, it
adopts a high tariff and inbound quota system as its weapon. For

General He Yaozu

fostering new industries, it uses an import tax for raw materials and machinery as its means. It also fears that the country's economy will be controlled by foreigners. Kemal even initiated the "Turkish Economic Fair," where the chairman, all local and central governments, chambers of commerce and industry, schools, banks, etc., all participated, and its oath is as follows:

1. The people of Turkey must abide by the agreement and should have a certain way of life.

2. The products of the country should be understood by the people, and the people using the country's products as much as possible is an obligation.

3. Increase domestic industrial production and improve its quality.

4. Make domestic manufactured goods cheap and try to promote their markets.

5. As much as possible, stop purchasing goods from foreign countries.

6. The central and local governments and all public agencies have reduced the need for imported goods to a minimum.

7. For foreign commodities, a domestic product substitution system should be implemented.

8. Sustain domestic industry and agriculture.

9. The government has aimed at promoting the purchase of products from domestic producers by introducing a new procurement law. And even if the same domestic product is up to 10% more expensive than its foreign correspondence, public institutions will prefer to buy the domestic one.

10. This Council shall establish branches in all provinces. The

management of its leadership shall be the responsibility of local governments and public agencies.

11. Exchange transactions should be strictly managed.

12. Production and consumption cooperatives should be organized.

13. The association encourages various bodies, student cooperatives, etc., to promote people to use domestic goods.

Turkish industry, promoted by the protection of the country and its people, has grown flourishingly and has developed without a break. Now the manufacturing of textiles, shoes, sugar, oil, paper, bricks, cement, etc., and the industries for food, clothing, and housing have gradually developed. There are two-three among these that have no fear of foreign competition. Since the expansion of agricultural products, they have been replaced by five-year plans for heavy industries such as iron, steel, mining, and chemical industries and the necessary machine industry. Transportation is also in the plan. Due to the painful experiences in the military affairs, after meeting the military needs, heavy railroad construction has been emphasized. The new government gradually withdrew foreign investors and constructed over 1,600 kilometers of railroads. A total of more than 280 million Turkish pounds was spent, without foreign investment and all by national treasury. So now Turkey has four necessities: food, clothing, housing, and transportation. Soon, it will be completely self-sufficient. Turkish territory is sparsely populated, so new policies have been implemented; poor people can take loans from the government and cultivate the land. Therefore, there are very few people who are unemployed. The progress in national economic construction and the general improvement in the standard of living of the people, needless to say, are reasons why Turkey is not affected by Communism. In short, the Turks are physically sound, faithful, practical, orderly, and obedient. Therefore, with their good leader, whether politically, economically, or ideologically, they feel sound and rational anytime, anywhere. This is a characteristic of modern Turkish politics.

The above all seem to coincide with our country's Three Principles of the People. This is enough to prove that the Premier's knowledge is very far-sighted, and his theory is correct. Recalling the time of going abroad, the differences between the two countries in the Central Party Office were reported. The Premier's ideas have given me confidence that we do not have to follow the old ideas. If we can implement new ones, then the Chinese nation will inevitably be liberated. This is demonstrated by the example of Turkey's success.

CHAPTER 5

The Turkish Diary of Hu Shiqing

A Brief Biography of Hu Shiqing

Hu Shiqing was a native of the Henan province and was born on October 31, 1880.[xxviii] A prominent educationist and philanthropist, he wrote extensively on different philosophical issues and travelogues.[xxvix] He traveled to numerous countries around the globe and published his experiences in various newspapers and magazines. Later, in 1933, he published his travelogues in a two-volumes set.[xxx] His travelogue on Turkey is the first account of the newly established Republic of Turkey written by a Chinese intellectual.

Turkey Diary[xxxi]

On March [1924] 16 at 3 pm, I got on board. The boat's name was *Leopolis*. The Ship belongs to Italian Lloyd Trieste Co. (Italia Maritime). Trieste before the war was an Austrian coastal city and after the war it was cut off from Austria and given to Italy. Before the war, Trieste was part of Austria and was a seaside town on the southern borders of the country. After the war, it was given to Italy. So, the company, along with the town, became Italy's. There were not many first-class passengers on board, so everyone could have large room

熱心贊助本院之
胡石青先生

Hu Shiqing

for themselves. At 8 o'clock in the evening, the ship sailed. I was incredibly bored. So, I slept early. At night, the ship started to sway heavily; I was exhausted and wanted to vomit.

On March 17, the northern wind blew strongly that day, and the sea was full of waves. The ship could only sail at 6 miles per hour; the crew could not see even the closest things because of the wind and the waves. There was an Argentinian professor of architecture who was also traveling; I started to chat with him. He told me that he had traveled to Beijing and was fascinated by the architecture there. There was also a German called Repnow; this gentleman had been in China for seven years and also loved to talk. So, it was not silent at all. I vomited three times. Later, the wind calmed down; I slept early.

March 18, in the morning, the boat anchored at the Dardanelles Strait. We should have arrived there last night, but were delayed because of the wind. The strait is narrow and long and flanked on the left and right by the mountains. There were not a lot of trees, which must have been destroyed by nature. The coastal city is named after the strait and is not very big. The buildings do not seem so bad. The boat stopped for a few hours and I did not get off. In the afternoon I read some books, took notes in my diary and chatted; it was pleasant. The Dardanelles was 167 miles away from Constantinople; and the strait was broad. The name of the sea was the Marmara Sea. The sea was calm. Amidst the mountains, it was like sailing in a lake. A delightful feeling.

On March 19, in the early morning, the ship already set sail for the Constantinople Strait. The cross-strait city was picturesque. The ship should have arrived yesterday morning. I had bought a ticket for the Romanian ship, and it should be arriving this morning. I wanted to save time and changed my ticket for this boat. However, the outcome was different. I spent more than ten yuan to save a day but had to stay a day more on the boat and suffered more from sea-sickness. The Romanian ship set sail a day later, and there was no wind or waves all the way. The ship arrived at the same time. Things cannot be predicted easily beforehand, even the small details. When getting off the ship, the porter and others could not speak any foreign languages, so there were translators—cheaters and very foxy—their mouths are full of the word of God; they are all damn forgers, their children and grandchildren are also included. In fact, all they say are deceitful. I spent almost 9 Turkish Pounds to get to hotel from the ship; it is equal to more than 10 Chinese yuan. The seaport is not far from the hotel, and all of the carriages were single. It is that expensive because some of the money goes to the city crown.[17] (By doing so), the Turks cannot earn the sympathy of other nations. This is also one of the reasons. In Pera Palace, a room without a bathroom, costs eight Chinese yuan—also oddly expensive. However, it was opened by non-Turkish people. I briefly took notes in my diary. At lunchtime, I met two Japanese men. One of them named Kinoshita Tōsaku worked as a medical professor for fifteen years and now works as a journalist for an English news outlet. The other one is a staff member of the South Manchurian Railway Co. and lives in Dalian. It was a delightful talk. The Japanese embassy supplied cars for their use. They firmly invited me to travel together; I thanked them and de-clined their offer. I read the city guide in the afternoon, felt weary at

---

17. Refers to municipality.

5 o'clock, and went out to street to have a walk. This city is divided into three major areas. The Bosphorus Strait, by the north Marmara Sea; the eastern part is the Black Sea. The Western Bank has a small, slice of the bay shaped like a horn; it is called the Golden Horn. The Golden Horn is divided into two by the west coast, forming a southern and northern bay. The southern part is called Stamboul (Istanbul), the city's most ancient and important place. The northern shore is called Galata Pera. Galata Pera is inhabited mostly by Europeans; it is also a business district. The east of the strait is the Golden Horn. To the west with a sharp angle lies Scutari (Üsküdar), the third part of the city. The western shore divides into two. Across the bay there are two bridges connecting the two shores. The east coast can be reached without the bridge. The hotel I stayed in was in the second district and named Pera Palace. Leaving the hotel, the first street is the most desolate one. Lanes are narrow, roads are made of stone and extremely uneven, and the residents are poor. Gradually, one gets into the firewood area. There is a turnaround. This city is rugged with mountains; small streets connect to the main streets, and streets mostly run from high to low. The main street has a tramway lane heading to the south and connects to the Golden Horn. The shore has two bridges, not far apart. The one to the west is called as the Old Bridge, and the one to the east is called as the New Bridge. I have crossed the New Bridge.

On each side of the bridge on both sides of the sidewalk there are five people standing, in white clothes and with a purple cloth covering their waist and holding a bronze money collection box.

Each person crossing the bridge must pay a Piastre (kurush). I did not have any cash with me; with a small ticket easily purchased from a small place by the side one can also cross the bridge. This (ticket) also covers the bridge fee. Provisional taxes as such are not the way to progress. The collectors stand there, and the people who cross the bridge give them the money, but some can also cross without paying. It is easy to make mistakes. At all public places in Italy when collectors take your money, they give you a receipt (ticket) and it gets stamped. The bridge is majestic; on both sides there are multiple staircases, and pedestrians can get on and off the ships here. In the middle of the bridge there are pontoons, which are still decorated with stone pavement. The tramway comes and goes. After the bridge, the Senta Sophia (Hagia Sophia) was built in the year 325. The Great Emperor Constantine built the church and praised it as the center of East Rome or the capital of Byzantine, and this building became the basis of the architecture. Compared with the Roman or Greek ones, this one is more splendid. In the year 404, half of it was destroyed in a fire. In the year of 532 it was completely destroyed in a fire again, and in the year of 548 restored again. It is solemn and beautiful; all architectural artists praise it. By the year 1453, the great heroic sultan of the Turks, Mehmed II, conquered Istanbul. After the conquest, he respected and protected the church and only removed the statues of Jesus, etc. and replaced them with the Quran and the Turkish flag. And this East Roman Church then became the first mosque of the new Turkish capital. I simply looked around; because I do not have any information about Islam and could not speak the language, I did not dare to go in. After the Church, there is a street not so far away and a bazaar. Muslims love trade; they all shout, though people cannot understand even a word of what they are shouting about. The bazaar was extremely irregular; most of them [the shopkeepers] sit on the floor cross-legged; they are very similar to the Muslim poor of China and are almost indistinguishable. The teahouses are also very similar to those of the Chinese Muslims. The poverty on this shore is the same or even worse compared to the other shore. I went back into the street. From the same way I crossed the bridge and returned to my hotel.

After dinner, I chatted with the two Japanese men. They came to my room and left at 11 o'clock. During my travels, these two Japanese gentlemen were very kind to me as a Chinese.

March 20, in the morning, I read some books and took some notes in my diary. The history of this place is the richest and the most interesting of all. During the daytime, I did not have chance to read the history of this city. In the afternoon, I searched for a local Muslim guide; he was wearing a veteran's badge. I talked with him and found out that he had served in the military, he was old and wounded during the war, and retired with a veteran's pension. But, the pension was not enough for his livelihood , and his house was destroyed by a fire during the first World War and still was not repaired. While we were talking, he understood that I was from China. He told me that 20 years ago, he went to China, Tian Shan, and Kashgar with a Hungarian delegation. He said his grandmother was Chinese and from the Yunnan province, his grandfather was an army general, and so on. His words were endless and not credible. We first took the carriage and passed the bridge that went to the church that I had been to yesterday. He told me that this church was not the Hagia Sophia, but one called the Yeni Cami Mosque. The Mosque of Yeni Cami; mosque in Turkish is called as the Cami. We went inside to have a look. When we went in, the doorkeepers gave us slippers that they wanted us to wear. The architectural pattern of the mosque was as such: in the middle, there was a curtain, and to the left and right there were semicircles. Surrounded by a large pillar corridor, the roof was arc-shaped, similar to western Europe's Gothic style, but the columns seemed different. Out of this hall, on the left-hand side, there was a huge gate. This gate was called the Gate of the Sultan; when the sultan came to pray he would use this gate. The sultan is the supreme emperor of the Muslims. So the Muslims who speak different languages sometimes address the sultan as emperor. The Yeni Cami looks like a little bigger than the Hagia Sophia, but they both are similar in form. Before going in, one has to put on the slippers first. The carpets on the floor were more than 400 years old. Men and women who come to pray first need to take off their shoes and go inside barefoot or with just the socks on. The chanting and prayers are so melodious. It is very similar to the Catholic chants and prayers in China. The Muslim chanting consists of eight parts, and I do not know why. This temple is the earliest ancestor of Byzantine architecture.

Today, the so-called "Roman style" of Romanesque is not the ancient Roman style but the Byzantine style; the curtains also make [the interior] look even higher. The Ancient Roman style is mostly Greek style. Departing this church [one finds] the Roman Hippodrome. Today, it is the most solemn part of the city. Surrounded by magnificent buildings, there is a park right in the center. In the garden, there is an ancient Greek snake monument: Serpent Column, three snakes entangled in each other. From the bottom to the top, it is tens of feet long. This monument was made by the ancient Greek people three thousand years ago. The emperor of Rome moved it here. Today, the three snakes' heads do not exist. Only the bodies remain. One of the heads is in a local museum, another is kept in a British museum, and the third one was lost long time ago. According to a legend, Mehmed II, after conquering the city, suspected that the monument was the soul of the Byzantine Empire and cut off its heads with his sword. I do not know if this is true or not. There is another monument from Egypt; it is also a majestic one but not Roman. Another monument is from [Kaiser] Wilhelm, a pavilion; it is also called the Kaiser Pavilion. Twenty years ago, the German emperor came [to Istanbul] and presented this special gift symbolizing the friendship and good relations between Germany and Turkey. This happened before the First World War. The other side of the park is the Sultan Ochmed Mosque (Sultanahmet Mosque/Blue Mosque); it is grander than the Hagia Sophia. Inside, there are very few square pillars and four gigantic round pillars. I have never seen such architecture in any other buildings. There are stripes up and down the pillars, something entirely different from the Greek style. The outer part of the stripes of the first one is sharp and inside of it there is a circle; the interior is also sharp, and outside there are circles, and the second one connects to the top. I counted all of them: every pillar has 30 stripes; between each of them there is 1 foot and 5 inches of space. The pillar is 50 feet tall and 18 feet wide and can be described as very big. Leaving the mosque, one sees the National Museum.[18] The sculptures are the most famous in the museum. I have seen beautiful carvings, and the Greeks are the most [beautiful]. The land of the Greek culture gradually came under Roman rule in the second century, and in the twelfth century, it gradually came under the Turk-

---

18. He must be referring to Istanbul Archeological Museum.

ish rule. In the fifteenth and sixteenth centuries, it was entirely controlled by the Turks. Every country's national museum has started to collect artifacts recently, so artifacts within the Turkish territory have also been sought recently. The most famous artifact is Alexander the Great's sarcophagus. There is almost no place for him inside this sarcophagus,. Alexander the Great's sarcophagus is made of resolute white marble and is 10 feet long. There is a ridge on top, like a roof which is 10 feet high. The carvings are exquisite, and during the excavation, it did not take any damage, which is also very rare. Whether the corpse in the sarcophagus belongs to Alexander the Great or not remains a controversy between archaeologists, but there is no doubt that it is a unique artifact. His sarcophagus can be considered as an Asian general's coffin; he died in Far Asia suddenly, so his generals divided Asia Minor, which is why his grave was there. On the sarcophagus there are scenes from the Greco-Persian war carved. There is also a scene of Alexander the Great on the battlefield. The Greek soldiers are carved as naked; one hand holds a sword, and the other one holds a bronze shield. The Persian soldiers are carved with clothes on, neat and tidy. These kinds of statues can also be seen elsewhere. European people only benefitted from the clothes very recently. The museum is within the old Forbidden City, and its walls and blockhouses are very similar to the Chinese style. On the opposite side of the museum is the old palace where, in earlier times, Mehmed the Second resided. There is also a museum of weaponry here containing different types of centuries-old large cannons and almost all of them have historical significance. By observing these, you can understand how the Turks, a small tribe from the East, in some hundred years' time controlled the West Asia and swallowed the East Europe. These are big, 400-year-old cannons, all very well manufactured and mechanical in nature. If Europe did not have modern scientific inventions, they could never defeat the Turks. In the museum there are paintings of the late dynasty's famous generals. The local guide searched for his grandfather named Mouchtsy (Maohe Riqi / Mustafa?); his grandmother's name was Liang Ming who was from China's Yunnan [province]. In the courtyard of the museum building stand countless pieces of new scrap ordinance. He told me that all of them were seized from the British in 1915. The whole courtyard was hardly big enough to contain all of them. There is also a great iron chain; it is said that in ancient times it was stretched across the surface between the two towers at two opposite shores of the Bosphorus Strait to prevent enemies from entering. According to a book, there was a giant locking system between the tops of the two towers. With the iron chain between them, one could pass on it from one shore to the other. It did not seem credible to me. The tower on the Istanbul shore was part of the former Ministry of War building. Today, it is in the middle of the museum courtyard and serves as a watchtower. The tower is architecturally distinct, with a twenty-foot-high pillar and eight open doors. We then went to a Muslim beerhouse and had a few drinks. The beer was very dense and had powdered cinnamon sprinkled over it.[19] After that, we went to the tomb of Mehmed II. The tomb was beside the mosque and was built at the same time as the mosque. Heroes do things in such ways. Outside of the tomb there is a huge pavilion and a white marble cof-

---

19. He must be talking about a traditional Turkish soft drink called *boza* (fermented millet drink). While *boza* has a very small amount of alcohol in it, it can be regarded as a soft drink.

fin 2–3 feet long and more than 1 foot wide. It was surrounded by kneeling and praying women who seemed very pious. It has been 400 years or so since Mehmed's death. The praying people must not wish for his soul to ascend to heaven early, so they covered his body with the coffin and pray. The local guide loves to say whatever we see is the largest in the world but, indeed, this tomb is the largest I have seen until now. The mosque of Mehmed II is also huge. In front of dozens of galleries and inside the walls there are giant pillars; before the main gate there are closed doors on the right and left sides. At the center of the courtyard there is an octagonal water pavilion with an octagonal pool that retains and is also surrounded by water. There is a central pool at the base. When people first come in, they wash their feet, mouths and faces. The atmosphere is very oriental. There is another huge ancient church nearby. According to a legend, it is the first Christian church [built in Istanbul]. There is a roof decorated with mosaics and the walls are full of Christian drawings. The local guide tells me that Christians love to say that Muslim destructiveness is great but that this church has survived despite being under Muslim dominance for 400–500 years. He told me that his family often comes here to recite the Quran and has not damaged the images of Jesus on the walls. From here the old city walls can be seen. There is no doubt that the Roman Empire was great, but the city gate was very small. The Romans were like that. In China, there are bigger gates even in villages. The local guide pointed out the gate and said that the Emperor, the conqueror Mehmed II, came into the city through this gate after the conquest of the city. The last emperor of the Byzantine Empire, Paleologus, was killed by arrows and died on this watchtower when the city fell. Thus, he was on his way back to his residence. In the evening, we went to a Turkish Restaurant with the local guide. There was a heavy mutton smell, not an oriental flavor. After dinner, we went to the street and had some tea in a small Jewish teahouse. I was very tired. The local guide took me back to my hotel, and we talked all the way there. I read some books and slept. In the daytime I went to the tomb of Abdülhamid the Second and visited the surrounding streets. They were filled with debris. The local guide pointed and said that it was all destroyed by the British bombardment in 1915 and thousands of families were killed. Mehmed's[20] tomb and mosque did not get any damage. The Muslims worship and believe in ancient sultans as deities, so it can be said that the God must also have protected them. I added some notes to my diary.

March 21, morning. I was thinking about the situation of the European War[21]; there is no book on this topic. There are only some war diaries written by the British about Gallipoli. During the war, Germany and Turkey incited and supported locals from Afghanistan to India to fight against the British. Although it was not something easy to achieve, the British feared the possibility and attacked the Turkish forces. In addition to the British Navy, the British also assigned Australian and New Zealand coalition forces for this attack. On April 25, 1915, they landed on the Gallipoli Peninsula. The West of the peninsula is the Aegean Sea, and the Dardanelles Strait is to the east. The strait is only 50 miles long, and the northeast is the narrowest part and not more than four or five miles in width. British,

---

20. Must be referring to Mehmed II. Mehmed is the Turkish version of Muhammad.

21. First World War.

Australian, and New Zealand coalition forces from the west landed at Suvla (Eceabat), occupied the Anzac Mountain and the Cape of Helles, the south of the peninsula. These three places were approximately 25 miles apart from each other. The Turks moved their army and resisted the British Army. The British could not advance and sometimes were defeated and once lost more than 7000 men. Australian and New Zealand coalition forces dared to fight, and the British twenty-ninth division defending Suvla were delayed and did not dare to attack or to enter, so the coalition forces lost the opportunity to attack. On August 9, British General Sir Alex Hamilton came for inspection and ordered an attack. The Turkish army hit back fiercely, and the British army was defeated. Moreover, their base in Suvla was captured by the Turkish Army. After that, the British Army's progress was much more difficult, until November 27, when the famous British General Lord Kitchener came for inspection and understood that there was no way to progress. By December 23, the whole Ottoman army retreated. Later, the British forces attacked and occupied the weak points of the empire such as Palestine and Mesopotamia. But they did not dare to attack Constantinople. Moreover, at that time, Turkey was a humble country surrounded by enemies. A huge British naval and land force landed on its shores. After eight months, the British could get into the Dardanelles Strait. From that point on, the British forces and the resisting Turkish forces were identified. Some parts of the city were destroyed by the bombardment; there is, too, much British artillery exhibited in the Military Museum.

I took some notes in my diary in the afternoon. Today is Friday which is the resting day for Muslims. The shopkeepers of other religions also close down their shops and comply with the rules of the country. The Turkish government, in doing business with Christian countries, respects their laws and declared Sunday as a holiday. Back then, the European powers decided that this region [Istanbul] should be under the control of the League of Nations. Now the sovereignty [of the city] wholly belongs to the Turkish government. Today there is a dancing party in the hotel, and there is a dancing tour of the hotel. The Governor General of Constantinople was also invited, and the announcement was placed outside of the hotel gate. The announcement was written in Turkish and French. If one wants to stay for more than fifteen days and wishes to travel the city, that person must go to the police station and obtain a permit. Diplomats and consuls are not included; their servants handle the paperwork for them. No matter who comes to the city and gets off the boat, they must first go to the police station and register with their passports. However, when you get off the boat, the police station and the tax clearance department are in the same big hall, so it is very convenient. When traveling to another country, always have a feeling of restraint. Often I have a feeling of weakness abroad as a Chinese. Now my feelings are between strength and weakness, and things are in a better direction. But my country blushes with shame when compared to Turkey. I hope the future generations of China will endeavor to be a strong nation.

After the dinner, we went to the small Jewish teahouse and had a cup of tea. There is a small Russian theater next to the hotel. One can have tea, food, etc., and can go inside to watch the shows by buying a ticket. The music and dance are vulgar and tedious, and all in French. Here, after the Turkish language, French is the most popular language. I watched the show for more than ten minutes and went back to my room and slept.

March 22, morning. I read some book cursorily. I bought some new books and photos. I walked around the city and had something to eat. When I came back, it was almost night time. An English newspaper reported about a place, Mersin (Tarsus). An American missionary school there did not comply with the local laws that require the local language and history classes to be taught by the local teachers. It was given a warning by the local board of education, and it did not respond, so it was ordered to be shut down the day before yesterday. Chinese people should see these actions and be ashamed. The English newspaper is called the *Orient News* and is published in this city.

In the evening, I had dinner at the small Russian theater; it was costly. After dinner, I went back to the hotel. Today, the hotel has a special dance occasion; famous men and women gather together to dance in an American style called Zozy. The ticket fare was two yuan. The audience also danced. From 10 to 12 o'clock, people were all together, three halls interconnected, with more than a thousand people watching. People passed through the halls and danced. The Zozy dance was going to start after an hour; I could not wait for it and went back to my room and slept.

March 23. At 5:30 in the morning, I woke up. Music and applause woke me up, and I could not fall back sleep. I got out of bed at 6:30. I quickly checked my luggage. Today I am going to Angora (Ankara). At 7 o'clock I left the hotel by a horse carriage, and went to the Istanbul Bridge [it is called the new bridge]. I got on the ship. There were so many porters who help you carry your luggage. First, I took the ship to go to the east side of the coast. The port at the east coast side was very crowded. I got off the ship and went to the train station. Again, they checked my passport. If you do not have the signature of the police, you cannot purchase the ticket. The porter there waited with me for half an hour, but I could not purchase the ticket. I went to the restaurant in the train station and gave the porter a Turkish lira equal to a yuan and two jiao of Chinese money, but he still disagreed with me endlessly over the money I should have given him. On the boat coming here, there was an Albanian lady. We sat in the same room and talked for a while in English. European women speak more foreign languages than men do. In Napoli, when I went to see the Mount Vesuvius, there was a German lady who later translated for me there. I have had such cases a lot. In the restaurant, there were only employees from a particular hotel. The name of the hotel is Oriental Hotel. It is one of the largest hotels on that side. The owners of this eccentric hotel were a couple, and all employees were Armenians. I hired a carriage to tour the northern part which consists of three districts: the first one is Haidar Pasha. This is where trains that go to Ankara is located; the second one is Kadi Keni (Kadıköy); and the third one is Moda. These are the Asian parts of Constantinople. I traveled for almost two hours. There is a small peninsula in the southern part, and there is a castle on it. I went back to the station and had lunch. After lunch I got on the ship and went back to the police station in Istanbul to have my passport stamped. They told me that diplomatic passports had to be stamped by the foreign affairs department of the city governorate. Then, I went to the city governorate and met the foreign affairs director, Adnan Bey. He signed the papers; I waited in the lounge approximately for 20 minutes, and my passport was signed. I gave a Turkish lira to the servants for their hospitality. The lounge was magnificent; it must have been the former Ministry of Foreign Affairs of Turkey. From the lounge, the palace can be seen. After leaving there, I looked to the palace for some time and also saw the museums I visited. I looked at the main gate of the palace; it was not open. The city walls overlook the sea. The eastern part of Europe overlooks the Bosphorus Strait, and the opposite side is Üsküdar. To the north is the Black Sea; south is the Marmara Sea. Such a beautiful scenery. When Constantine moved his capital here, he had his reasons. I went back and got out of the city gate. On the street, I bought some food for the next day. I then crossed the strait and went to the eastern coast. Again, I had my dinner at the train station and went back to the hotel and slept. The hotel was open for Christians, but there were also Muslims staying. There were even some Muslim women staying.

March 24. In the morning I went to the train station and had breakfast. The restaurant prepared soup with meatballs, fruit, and so on for me. I purchased my ticket and got on the train carrying my luggage and food. I shared a room with two people, one of whom was from Bulgaria. His name was Pereff, and he was the former consul general in Constantinople. He could speak some English. There were military officers on the train checking passports and registration. They all speak Turkish, so he helped me with the translation. It was quite moving. The two men seemed like Germans and looked like officials; they also had their passports from the police station. Around 11 o'clock, each of us took out our food and had our breakfast. We passed through the fertile lands; the color of the soil turned red; in English it is called clay loam, meaning soft clay fields; the name of Henan province in China is also associated with such soil. These kinds of fields are the finest. The cultivation of such fields is very complicated, and crop failures occur very often. At 1 o'clock in the afternoon we arrived in İzmit. The name of the city comes from the İzmit Bay. During the Greco-Turkish War, this place was the Turkish National Army's stronghold. We went further toward the south-east. The south of the road there were mountains, on the northern side, a lake. The scenery was outstanding. The soil here was more blackish and fertile. There was a freshly dug place, and the strata of the soil could be seen. The upper layer of the soil contained water from the forest, and snowmelt runoff from the mountains collected. Even the leaves from the trees become soil in time. The rainfall must be so much that it comes down from the mountains and forest. And the fields were not well cultivated, so they are in this situation. The northern side was full of such fields. Around 3 o'clock, the road led to the mountains; there were caves. At 4 o'clock, we crossed the Sangarins (Sakarya) River bridge. The bridge was destroyed by the Greek Army during the Greco-Turkish war. After crossing the bridge, we sometimes saw mountains, sometimes plains, and saw fewer and fewer people outside. At 10 o'clock in the evening, we arrived in Eski Shehr (Eskişehir), the junction of the national railways from south to the north and a strategic place. Before the Roman forces arrived, Dorylaeum (Karacahisar) was the ruler of this city. There were antiquities an hour and a half away, but it was already midnight, so I did not dare to leave the station. Instead, in the train station I had some soup, drank tea, and rested for a while. The people of the city did not look like the Orientals; this city is not like the East. There was only one small shop, and the ones who worked there looked like Mongolians. At 11:30 the train moved on. I sat down and slept. Fortunately, it was not cold.

March 25. After dawn, at 7 o'clock, I woke up and did not sleep again. I went to the bathroom to wash my face. The women sitting in the third class also came to wash their faces. They did not wait for the ones inside to come out before they rushed in. I was standing there waiting and could not go in. I did not have breakfast today. Further to the east, the people are poorer. The houses in the villages are 10 feet high with a flat roof and small windows not larger than two feet square. It seems that the fields are not well cultivated, and there are more barren fields. At 11 o'clock we arrived in Ankara, and I got off the train. Pereff and I took the same carriage and went to Hasan Bey. He was familiar with the Turkish language, so we did not have any obstacles. The two of us shared the same room. This room was recently repaired, and both the ceiling and the floors were painted. After a little rest, we had breakfast. The food was European style; the smell was not as heavy as back in Constantinople.[22] In the hotel, there were people who can speak some French, but no one could speak any English. In the afternoon, I went with Pereff to the Grand National Assembly to visit some friends. When I was in Hungary I received a letter of introduction from Professor Prohle, and I visited Colonel Mahmud Nedim Bey[23] the deputy of Malatya. Today, he was not going to come to the assembly, so I left my letter of introduction and name card with the doorman. He asked me to wait for a while, but my waiting was completed without any information. The National Assembly is a new building; its scale is very small, and its surrounding walls were not completed. There were some long wooden stools in the waiting room for people waiting for their ap-

---

22. Fishy smell. Ankara is far away from the sea. Therefore, there is no sea smell.

23. Mahmud Nedim Zabcı (1882–1955).

pointments. I took my time and walked around and went to the column of Julian. Julian was one of the rulers of ancient Rome. He is known to historians for his talent in martial arts, literature and arts. In the second and third centuries A.D., he was the last emperor who did not believe in Christianity. Moreover, the former emperor was mediocre and believed in Christianity; his relatives were also mostly believers. When he attacked Persia in the East, he suddenly died on the way, just like the Macedonian Alexander the Great's death while he was attacking the East. This place initially belonged to the Persians so he had this monument erected here. Not far from the monument is the Roman Temple of Augustus. He was a hero; the Romans worshipped him like a god, so there is a temple for him. The monument was built purely in Roman style. The temple will be renovated since it almost cannot be identified as a Roman ruin. These antique Roman artifacts must be the ones farthest to the East. Only half of the top of the monument was intact. There is a bird's nest on the top and army tents next to the monument; it looks awkward. From there I went to the street and toured the old part of the town. There were old-style small shops everywhere. There were some shoe polishers in the street; people with proper shoes were rare. The poor class people mostly have low noses. Caucasians were the majority of the soldiers; they have high noses and their faces were blackish, purplish, and chaff colors. There were so many beggars. After touring around, I went back to the parliament. They told me Nedim Bey was not going to come today. In the evening, I went back to the parliament and gave the gatekeeper 60 kurush to have him hand over the letter. After dinner, I slept early.

On March 26, early in the morning, I went to the Ministry of Foreign Affairs to inquire whether I needed to get my passport stamped again or not. Later on, I went back to the parliament and asked for a meeting with Nedim Bey at 1 o'clock in the afternoon. I had already toured the city and understood its terrain. Because of the terrain, the oldest part of the city is on the mountain. The laborers turn mountains into streets. The newest part of the city is at the foot of the mountains where the government offices and the parliament are located. The train station is a few miles away. The station is in the middle of a small plain, and it seems that it will designate a new route in the future. It was supposed to be a crossroad with two main parts; this place will be an important part of the new city in the future without any doubt. I went to the street and drank some tea at a teahouse and also smoked a Turkish hookah. The hookah consists of three parts; the lower part is a glass pot with some boiling water in it. The upper part is the smoke pot, as big as a small teacup with a magnetic bottom and a copper inlay at the top that looks like a grate. The pot has a long tube connected downwards. Beside that there is rubber pipette longer than three feet, and one end of it is screwed to the pot and the other is for inhaling the smoke. All the parts can be folded away and cleaned with a brush. When smoking the tobacco leaves they are covered with charcoal fire. One should inhale it with his all strength in order to smoke it for a long time. I could not smoke it anymore. Also, I could not taste the smoke. People on the street and in the teahouse, including kids, were all talking to me. The kids and I greeted each other and laughed together. I went back to the hotel and had lunch. I exchanged British pounds to local money at the hotel. At about 1 o'clock in the afternoon, I went to the parliament again to visit Nedim Bey. He could not speak English; he called someone to help with the translation. We talked until the parliament session opened, and he gave me permission to listen to the session. Later on, they started to talk about the military budget, and it was the secret part, so I left and waited until the secret session ended. Nedim Bey met me at the gate and appointed another time to meet again. The parliament hall was very modest and had two gates in total. The listeners and parliamentarians all use the same gates to enter and exit. The listeners sit in the seat section located above the columns. Eighty to ninety percent of the parliamentarians were present, and among them there were many elder ones. There are around ten parliamentarians with their white turbans; these people are from the old faction. There are many such people back in Xinjiang. I came out of the parliament and then went to a small teahouse. A few people could speak some French. We talked for some time, but it was difficult to understand them. I went back to the hotel. At 7 o'clock in the evening, Nedim Bey, along with the translator, came and took me to a restaurant for dinner. We talked until 10 in the evening. I asked him some questions as follows:

The first question was, after the abolishment of the caliphate, was there a possibility of a new organization to bring the Muslim countries together?

His answer was that, after the abolishment of caliphate, only political aspects of the matter should be improved, nothing more may come in the aftermath. Outsiders often misunderstand the caliphate and the political issues, but for improvements the abolishment was inevitable. For instance, judicial reform must be carried out as urgently as today, and the religious court cannot have authority anymore. The government is determined about it. The judiciary is an

example like the other issues. The country is not without conservatives and people with a wait-and-see attitude. After the abolishment
of the caliphate, the nation lost interest in the matter. The abolition
and everything else went hand in hand. For the Muslim countries
to have a common purpose and to have a union, they must all have
a common enemy, and this is the British. In short, the foundation
of the caliphate is already dead, and there is no chance of resurrec-
tion. There is no hindrance to interrelationships between Muslim
countries.

The second question: Muslims do not eat pork. Is this because of
the same reasons in Christianity and Judaism?[24] Is this practice still
in compliance with the past?

The answer: people can be roughly divided into three groups. The
first group is strictly keeping with religious rules and does not eat
pork. The second group does not keep with religious regulations and
eats pork. The third group is not religious but, as a habit, does not
eat pork. However, Muslims mostly rely on animal husbandry for a
living. Raising pigs, slaughtering and selling pork is also a part of
animal husbandry. Within our territories there so many Christians
who do eat pork.

The third question: the British want the Iraqi king to be the caliph.
Do you think this is something you need to take precautions for?

His answer: this cannot be successful. In Egypt, Persia, India, there
is no lack of knowledgeable people. They will never admit the king
of Iraq as their leader and fall into the British snare. There is no need
to talk about the Turkish response. He asked me about the political

---

24. The author apparently thinks that eating pork is also prohibited in Christianity.

and diplomatic situation of Muslims in China. I told him whatever I knew. In the end, he asked me about the breaking situation between China and Russia and whether it can lead to a war. I answered: Russia wants to invade Outer Mongolia. They will organize an election in Outer Mongolia before invading and will use it as an excuse to do so. Great Britain and Italy recognized it as an independent country; Karakhan's attitude suddenly changed, and I think this is the main reason that negotiations broke off. However, both China and Russia are in a period of recuperation and development; I think both will never declare a war. He talked about the situation in Xinjiang; his words were like the Russians. Someone wanted to talk to him, but he seemed like he did not want to talk to that person.

There were no separate rooms in the hall; there was a big banquet there. He told me that a Russian economic commissioner wanted to purchase Turkish goods. I do not know the nature of these Russian people. The Russians have had desires in Xinjiang for a long time; it was unknown what was going to happen to the boundaries of Europe, Great Britain, and Italy and more broadly in the East. After this meeting, Nedim Bey took me back to the hotel with a car.

March 27. I woke up early and took some notes in my diary. At 10 o'clock I went to the Parliament, and Nedim Bey introduced me to Djalal Noury (Celal Nuri),[25] the deputy of Gallipoli (Gelibolu). He could speak English, and we talked for half an hour. He introduced me to the chief of commerce who was going to help me with my questions on the economy. Because he had an important meeting,

---

25. Celal Nuri İleri (1881–1938), writer, politician and journalist, was an important figure of the late Ottoman and early Republican period.

we decided to meet again in the afternoon. I left the parliament building and headed to the ancient part of the city. Most of the old buildings were damaged; they were from Roman times or even earlier. The people's living conditions were too naive and unbearable. I went back to the hotel, had lunch, and wrote down three questions in English to ask in the afternoon. The translations are as follows.

My first question: What are the main parts and outline of the national budget?

My second question: What is the situation of distribution of land in your respective country? Do large-scale lands belong to landlords, get distributed to individuals, or do they belong to the state?

My third question: According to my personal experience in the Great European War (the First World War), we know that self-sufficiency in food production is as important as the independence of a nation in wartime. The relationship between the decline of British exports and then in its agricultural products is of such importance in the economic status of a nation. Does your government have a plan to reward agricultural progress?

In the afternoon, at 1:30 pm, I went to the parliament and waited shortly. Celal Nuri Bey, the deputy of Gallipoli, took me to the cabinet room. I talked to the chief of commerce. He told me that the country's agricultural lands are mostly small fragments, so it is cultivated by individuals, but in the eastern part of the country, there are landlords who own large chunks of agricultural land. The life of the nation must not rely on imports, but İstanbul has an extraordinary situation. For the improvement in agricultural production, Istanbul has to import machinery, and the recent, significant loss of population during the war makes these imports inevitable. The rest of the questions were going to be answered by Celal Nuri Bey by a letter on a later day. At 2 o'clock, he and the chief of commerce were going to attend a meeting. I left the parliament. The people of this country are very simple-minded and straightforward; when I talk to anyone they answer directly. On my visit to the chief of commerce, I raised three heavy and complicated questions to him. Later on, I realized that my questions lacked courtesy. Days of over-thinking on these problems have caused this loss. In the middle of my journey, exhausted, my energy has its limits so this is normal.

Yesterday, I asked the Ministry of Foreign Affairs about my passport, and they told me that there was no need for it to be signed again, but today the owner of the hotel told me it must be signed again. He let me go to the police station. They told me the diplomatic passports must be taken to the Ministry of Foreign Affairs. I went to the ministry again, and they told me there is no need to sign again. The presidential palace is a two-floor building in the shape of an "工" character, there are five windows in the center and the left and the right sides have three windows. The eaves are slightly colorful. It stands on two blocks. The left-hand side is the presidential palace where Kemal put an end to the sultan's powers twice, including the abolition of the caliphate. Kemal repudiated the treaty with foreign forces, defeated Greece, recaptured three provinces in Europe, revoked the international condominium for the Dardanelles strait, forced the British and other foreign armies out of İstanbul, intimidated the British war time unbreakable iron cabinet, and deployed his operational troops. The right-hand side is a bit lower, and the eaves are more colorful. This is the president's residence, the place he lives with his wife Latiph (Latife). The residents of the city are very straightforward when asked. They answered directly that the left-hand side is Kemal's and the right-hand side is Latife's. The palace is located between the old and the new city centers and on a hill, looking toward a far distant scenery; the old buildings of the old city can be seen in the background. It also has a dignified and glorious atmosphere. For the new part of the city, this was the first new building to be built. When getting out of the hotel I stayed in, it can be seen. Only, I did not know it was the presidential building back then.

Kemal is forty-two or forty-three years old. For more than ten years he devoted himself to the country's affairs. In wartime, he was active and busy coping with the war. Always busy with military affairs, he could not think of having his own family before saving his country. So, over the years, he has always been single. Latife is a wealthy lady of good reputation, who could speak English, French, and German and who had traveled all over Europe, including two big cities such as London and Paris. She is 26 or 27 years old. In recent years, the Greek army collapsed, the negotiations at Lausanne were successful. Kemal achieved all of this, and he and Latife have had a happy marriage. They choose an auspicious marriage, at either Latife's house or her private apartment. I do not know for sure. Anyway, her name spread throughout the country.

This city is an ancient one. In the ancient times, it was called Ancyra (Ankara), and people have been living here since the ancient times. Now it is called Angora (Ankara). The modern name comes from the ancient one. Ancient Egyptian, Greek, and Roman antiques are still here and waiting for future generations to examine them. The first of the eastern nationalities to conquer this land was a branch of the Turks; the first Mongolian was Tamerlane (also called Timur), who during his march to the west defeated Sultan Bayezid here. Soon the Mongol presence receded; this city came under the Turkish rule again. Before the Turks came to this city, from the south the Persians and from the east Crusaders all rested their horses here. Osman [formerly known as the Ottoman] reinforced and made the city a center of long-term development. Since Mehmed II, the conqueror, moved the capital to Constantinople, the fame of this city gradually subsided. Four years ago, under the leadership of the great General Mustafa Kemal Grand the National Assembly of Turkey was established here. In the old times, the city was a glorious and a well-known place.

I went to the parliament; the soldiers were guarding the gate so I could not go in. There was a secret meeting.

After dinner, I sat down for a while and then slept, first, because there was no place worth going and, second, because the streets were all muddy. After dark, there are no lights, so even if one wants to take a walk, it is impossible.

March 28. I woke up early and had breakfast with Pereff. After the meal, I hired a car to go to the train station. The hotel let me go to the police station to show my passport; the police gave me a coupon. Without such a coupon, I cannot buy train tickets. I encountered a German gentleman, Otto Horre. He helped me. He was the director of the German locomotive factory. At 9 o'clock, I arrived at the station. 45 minutes later, I bought a ticket. By 10:30 the train started moving. This city is geographically in the center of the state, and the population nearby is very scarce and desolate. Agriculture and animal husbandry are the primary occupations, and mostly the women work. Animal husbandry is mostly conducted by children; men are scarce.

At 11 o'clock I again arrived at Eski-Shehr (Eskişehir), got off the train and had some tea. There were two parliamentarians in the same room with me. One could speak some English, and the other one could speak some French. Both were advocating the Latin alphabet reform in the parliament. We talked about the ruling party. They told me that the one-party system is only suitable for the nation-building and state-building process. After the peace, there must be at least two parties and so on. The night was sweltering; I slept where I sat.

March 29. At dawn, I arrived at the Sakarya River. For days, the weather was warm, so the snow on the mountains melted down, and the water of the river is now up a few feet. A few of the bridges on the river are now at the same level with the water. The train from İzmit was delayed until 2 p.m. From the north of İzmit to Üsküdar the entire way overlooks the sea. The richness never dies in this country. The scenery is beautiful. The wealthiest cities in this country are also on these coasts. Getting off the train, there were people who helped carry my luggage. I got out of the train station only carrying my handbag. I gave [the porter] one Turkish Lira and 20 kurush for that, but he said it was too few and threw it on the ground. Later on, I gave him an extra 50 kurush and left. These people are not professional at all. There were more luggage carriers than the incoming passengers. So, in a short time, such as a minute, by carrying a three-pound handbag, they earn enough money for 2–3 days. This is the same everywhere, not only at this train station. I crossed the strait and the Golden Horn Bridge, hired a car, and went to the Pera Palace Hotel. I took a long bath and got cleaned up. In the afternoon, I booked tickets for the ship. I found a small restaurant for dinner; it was cheap and delicious. I walked in the street, there were some people catching pheasants. Later on, I went back to the hotel and read some statistics about Turkey. I slept early.

March 30. I read some books and checked my clothes. At 11 o'clock, I went to the Ministry of Foreign Affairs to have my passport signed for leaving the country. This procedure is not necessary in other countries, but in this country, it is a must. This section was not the governorate's diplomatic division, but the Ministry of Foreign Affairs appointed its workers, and the coach drivers told me the man in charge was called Adnan Bey. Adnan Bey kept me waiting for ten minutes. Later on, I got my passport. In the room there were three Turkish women who talked with me about the recent trends in French. After leaving there, I headed to the museum again. Later on, I came back, found a small restaurant and had lunch. After the meal, I went to the street and bought two or three pieces of clothing and small table mats. These are the local products of the country. I bought a book, *Memories of a Turkish Statesman 1913–1919* by Djernal Pasha (Cemal Pasha), read it for a while, and then took notes in my diary.

March 31. Within this short time that I traveled through Turkey and tried to find a conclusion for my travel, I was not successful. I was tired and fell asleep. In the morning, I kept on thinking about the conclusion. The more I thought, the more the conclusion was being pushed back. I went out by 12 o'clock and bought a ticket for the ship. I had a meal outside and bought the book *Turkey, the Great Powers and the Bagdad Railway* by Edward Mead Earle. Earle was a professor of Columbia University. He had no prejudice toward any country in Europe, and he collected many secret treaties before and after the war for the research of this country. In my opinion, he is the best. I read it until very late at night. We had an appointment for dinner with the German gentleman Otto Horre who came here with me from Ankara. I had a feeling that in this country, people's faces have German characteristics and asked him whether he paid attention to or not. He told me that this is often a misunderstanding, and told me not to ask again because he could not know the answer either. For some reason, he could not answer the question. This matter is closely related to the study of heterogeneous marriages and may be a research question for future generations. Later on, I took a bath and slept.

April 1. I woke up in the morning, checked my luggage, looked at the map, went out, and had something to eat. I purchased an English newspaper called the *Orient News* and read it. The news was about how YMCA activities inland were to be banned because it is a religious organization, so it is not legal and cannot exist and so on.

In the afternoon I hired a car and took my luggage from the carriage to the small and then on to the bigger ship; I had different people to carry my luggage from one ship to the other and gave them money, one by one. From the car to the ship cost more than 20 Turkish liras. Later on, the man who carried luggage waited for someone who could speak English. I was talking to myself about how the man had his business for many days now and could not survive without the money. There are hundreds of people who have luggage to be carried in and out of the ship every day, but there are also thousands of people who wait to carry the luggage for a living. I am sure that if there were any factories to open here, none of them want to do this job.

The name of the boat was *Famaca*, and it belonged to the British

Khedivial Company. It weighs six thousand tons. During dinner, I talked with an old Hungarian man called Lonis Roth. After dinner, I read some books and slept at 11 o'clock.

On April 2, at dawn, the ship had already come out of the Dardanelles Strait. The breeze did not make me dizzy. However, the weather was not very clear. At around 6 o'clock in the afternoon, the ship arrived at Smyrna and anchored. This city is the second largest in Turkey and is located on a bay on the western side of Asia Minor. The name of the bay and the city was the same. In third class, there were around 200 Turks. They all got off the ship here, carrying complexly wrapped up bags. It looked like the same in China when people move their houses. When Lonis Roth disembarked from the boat, he found me and said goodbye. After dinner, I read some books and slept early.

On April 3, I woke up in the morning. After breakfast with an American car businessman and two British traveling women, I got on the ship. Last night, a Turkish police officer got on board. First, he wanted our passports and signed them. Today, the passports were checked by customs before we got off the ship. The crew of the small boat told me that because I am Chinese, they feel very close to me. I went on and off the ship, back and forth, twice. I paid a lira and a half in total. The price was fair. After we went ashore, the American businessman went to work, and the two British women and I hired a car together and toured the city, went to Bagus Mountain, and returned to the dock. The city is located between the port and the mountain; there is an ancient city in the mountains still intact, probably from the Eastern Roman time. It must have been built around 2000 years ago. There is a place in the mountains called Diana's

Bath, with numerous springs and a small pool within Roman walls. Some parts of these walls are still in good shape. The spring water is cold and still running. There is also a place called the Caravan Bridge not far away and not a big one. It was built 2000 years ago. The Koti Empire's royal road goes towards the west from here. It was the commercial center between Asia and the West. It is still here, and the history of the bridge is ancient. There is a bazaar in the city. In the year 1402 Tamerlane, the general of the Mongolian Army, moving westwards conquered this city; he brought stones from the top of the mountain. This place is very close to the castle of St. Peter from the Eastern Roman times. 20 years after Tamerlane's conquest, the city fell into the hands of Turks. Moreover, here, there is an ancient church called St. Polycarp. It is one of the seven churches in Asia, and it later on became the center of Christianity in Asia Minor. After hundreds of years, in 1920, by the Treaty of Sèvres, the British advocated that İzmir to be given to the Greeks. This city was the second largest in Turkey, it was the commercial center of Asia Minor, and it was the intersection and terminal point of all railways running from the north to the south. Before the war, the British were dominant in the city, and they did not want to invade the city directly, so they let the Greeks invade for their benefit. Greece used its army to invade the city while the British provided it with supplies and weapons. Back then, the Imperial Army collapsed and scattered, and the New National Army was not ready for a battle. British officers and commanders were commanding the Greek Army, and it reached deep into the east of the Sakarya River. Not long after, the National Army attacked the westwards. On August 1922, the Greek army was defeated and retreated, and the British commanders fled. The Turkish army re-entered the city on 13 September at 4:00 pm. A fire began in the Armenian Quarter, a district in the northeast of the city. After the fire began, there was a strong wind blowing from the south-east. The fire reached the sky and the west, mostly habited by the Europeans. The rich part of the city, the coastal area turned into ashes. The Turkish part of the city was in the south, and it was entirely well-preserved. The damage is estimated to be worth about 40 million British pounds; the casualty numbers are unknown. It was catastrophic. We completed the tour in the city at 11:30 went back to the dock, reclaimed our passports from the customs, got on a small boat, and went back to the ship.

At 5 o'clock in the evening we arrived at the Mytilene Island. It is the largest island along the coasts of Anatolia; half of it is inserted towards the Gulf of İzmir and after the war, it became a part of Greece. The island's scenery is extremely beautiful. I took some notes in my diary and did not get off the ship at the coast. The waves were as flat as a mirror; I slept early in the evening.

Glossary

Chinese	English
土耳其, 土國	Turkey
安古拉	Ankara
羅桑條約	Lausanne Treaty
巴黎	Paris
威尼斯	Venice
君士坦丁	Constantinople (Istanbul)
列強	Great Powers
外法權	Capitulations
希臘人	Greeks
阿美尼人	Armenians
猶太人	Jews
來波奴	Repnow
白拉宮	Pera Palace
木下東作	Kinoshita Tōsaku
小倉鐸二	Koichi Ogura
南滿鐵路本社	South Manchurian Railway Co.
包氏浮羅峽	Bosphorus
馬母拉	Marmara Sea
黑海	Black Sea
金角灣	Golden Horn
司坦堡	Stamboul (Istanbul)

加拉他白拉	Galata, Pera
土庫塔里	Scutari (Üsküdar)
聖蘇裴亞教棠	Hagia Sophia (Ayasofya)
穆哈默德第二	Mehmed II (Mehmed the Conqueror)
回教堂	Mosque
巴察	Bazaar (Kapalıçarşı)
天山	Tian Shan
喀什噶爾	Kashgar
葉尼扎迷冒司克	Yeni Cami Mosque
高狄氏	Gothic
卑參廷	Byzantine
羅馬式	Romanesque
維廉	Wilhelm
凱薩亭	Kaiser Pavilion
蘇丹阿喝默德冒司克	Sultan Ahmed Mosque (Blue Mosque)
古禁域	Forbidden City
毛喝日齊	Mouchtsy (Mustafa?)
梁明	Liang Ming
布氏浮羅	Bosphorus Strait
舊陸軍部	Old Ministry of War
耶蘇教	Christian
可蘭經	Quran
武皇	Emperor the conqueror
巴留婁古	Paleologus
哈默德第二	Abdülhamid II
歐戰	European War
噶里浦里	Gallipoli (Gelibolu)

澳洲新西蘭	Australia and New Zealand
愛珍海	Aegean Sea
韃靼海峽	Dardanelles Strait
穌夫拉	Suvla (Eceabat)
安察克	Anzac
希來角	Cape Helles
哈米屯	Sir Alex Hamilton
吉青納	Lord Kitchener
帕利司坦	Palestine
墨索波他米亞	Mesopotamia
歐洲各強	European Powers
國際聯盟	League of Nations
市政總督	Governor General
麥西納	Mersin/Tarsus
東方薪聞	*Orient News*
美國摘咨	Zozy Dance
昂葛拉	Angora (Ankara)
司坦堡穚	Istanbul Bridge
土爾基李耳	Turkish lira
阿爾般尼	Albania/Albanian
納波里	Napoli
微蘇飛火山	Mount Vesuvius
東方旅館	Oriental Hotel
阿門尼	Armenian
海大耳霞下	Haidar Pasha (Haydar Pasha)
喀的克威	Kadıköy
冒大	Moda
孔土但丁	Constantinople

阿德南伯	Adnan Bey
司庫塔利	Scutari (Üsküdar)
布爾加利	Bulgaria
白葉佛	Pereff
膠土軟田	Clay loam
河南	Henan
伊思米	Izmit
希土大戰	Greco-Turkish war
土國民軍	Turkish National Army
三家流	Sangarins (Sakarya)
埃土基色	Eski Shehr (Eskişehir)
多律留	Dorylaeum (Karacahisar)
哈三伯	Hasan Bey
國民大會	Grand National Assembly
蒲瑞列	Prohle
馬拉地洲代表納丁伯	Colonel Mahmud Nedim Bey deputy of Malatya
汝連高龍碑	The column de Julian
馬基頓亞列山大	Macedonian Alexander the Great
羅馬阿古司杜廟	Roman Temple of Augustus
喀里夫	Caliphate
教主	Caliph
伊拉克	Iraqi
外蒙	Outer Mongolia
喀拉汗	Lev Karakhan
加拉奴利	Djalal Noury (Celal Nuri)
商務總長	Chief of commerce
克馬爾	Kemal (Mustafa Kemal)

拉梯菲	Latiph (Latife)
偷敦	London
巴黎	Paris
洛桑	Lausanne
昂次拉	Ancyra (Ankara)
昂哥拉	Angora (Ankara)
塔木偷	Tamerlane
鐵木爾	Timur
蘇丹巴亞西	Sultan Bayezid
波斯	Persian
十字軍	The Crusaders
奧次門	Othman (Osman)
奧頭門	Ottoman
穆司他法克馬爾	Mustafa Kemal
侯佩	Otto Horre
姬馬爾霸下	Djernal Pasha (Cemal Pasha)
埃烈君	Edward Mead Earle
哥偷大學	Columbia University
耶教青年會	YMCA
法馬喀	Famaca
克的維公司	British Khedivial company
羅特	Lonis Roth
司米納	Smyrna (Izmir)
小亞西亞	Asia Minor
巴固山	Bagus mountain
狄阿納浴池	Diana Bath
路拉番橋	Caravan Bridge
古喀地帝國	Koti Empire

彼得壘宮	Castle of St. Peter
包里喀	St. Polycarp
亞洲七教堂	Seven Churches
塞佛會議	The Treaty of Sèvres
帝國軍隊	Imperial Army
新國民軍	New National Army
阿門尼街	Armenian Quarter
米地里尼	Mytilene
司米納	Smyrna (Izmir)
伊斯美帕沙	İsmet Pasha
國民黨	Nationalist Party – Kuomintang
戶口	Residence registrations
慕斯泰發凱末爾	Mustafa Kemal
土耳其國民黨	Turkish Nationalist Party
土國黨軍	Turkish Party Army
青年黨	Young Turk Party
安哥拉	Ankara
奧斯曼王朝	Ottoman Dynasty
亞得里那	Edirne
小亞細亚	Asia Minor
奧斯曼	Ottoman
空尼亞	Konya (Konia)
布魯撒	Bursa
東羅马帝國	East Roman Empire
波斯	Persians
阿拉伯人	Arabs
賽洛初克	Seljuks (Seljuq or Seljucide)
鐵木兒	Timur

蒙古人	Mongolians
塔庫辟斯	Trikoupis
巴路克巴杂	Balık Pazarı (Fish Bazaar)
大石汗札代司	Taşhan Caddesi (Taşhan Street)
遮目呼雷耶札代司	Cumhuriyet Caddesi (Republic Street)
買支利斯札代司	Meclis Caddesi (The National Assembly Street)
國務院	The State Council
昌克牙	Çankaya
戛滋	Gazi (The first teacher training school of Turkey)
大總統凱末爾將軍	Great General President Kemal
哈克迷耶特密利耶	Hakimiyet-i Milliye
大石汗	Taşhan
艾渥克夫	Ankara Palace
巴爾幹	Balkans
天主教的亞类尼亞	Catholic Armenians
回教禮拜堂	Mosque
哈芝巴以剌木	Hacı Bayram
烏庫斯特廟	Augustus Temple
克子塔石	Kız Taşı
蔣院長	Chiang Kai-shek
中華民族	Chinese Nation
土鎊	Turkish pounds
管子	Guan Zi
土耳其經濟儉約會	Turkish Economic Fair
民權主義	Democracy
阿拉托利亞	Anatolia

共產主義	Communism
泛回教的理想	Pan-Islamism
民族主義	Nationalism
孟德婁會議	Montreux Convention
法西嘶主義	Fascism
家族主義	Nepotism
宗族主義	Clannism
共和國民黨	Republican People's Party (CHP in Turkish)
復辟	Restorationists (Conservatives)
地方主義	Localists
守舊派	Conservatives
伊斯美將軍	İsmet Pasha

Notes

i. 梁启超, "中国与土耳其之异 (梁启超)," in 救亡 第*1*册, ed. 青溪散人, 1915, 29–48.

ii. 駐和陸大臣, "譯呈土耳其憲法由," n.d., 02-12-026-01-018.

iii. 和森, "祝土耳其國民黨的勝利," *Xiang Dao* - 向导, 1922, 期: 3 edition.

iv. 君宇, "土耳其國民軍勝利的國際價值," 向导, 1922.

v. 周慧平, "民国外交家施肇基," 民国档案, no. 2 (1992): 139.

vi. "臨時大總統令（中華民國元年四月初八日）：任命施肇基爲交通總長此令," 临时公报, 1912, 2.

vii. "交通部总长施肇基:[照片]," 中国革命记, 1912, 1.

viii. 周慧平, "民国外交家施肇基," 140.

ix. "大总统令:署外交总长施肇基因病恳请辞职," 交通丛报, 1923, 1–2.

x. 周慧平, "民国外交家施肇基," 141.

xi. 周慧平, 142.

xii. "施肇基在外交討論會演講：題爲遊歷土耳其之感想," 寰球中国学生会周刊, 1929, 1.

xiii. 施肇基, "土耳其漫游录," 军事杂志(南京), 1929; 施肇基, "游歷土耳其之感想," 世界周报, 1929; 施肇基, "游歷土耳其之感想," 新纪元周报, 1929; "施肇基在外交討論會演講：題爲遊歷土耳其之感想"; 施肇基, "游歷土耳其感想," *Shen Bao,* 申报, May 5, 1929.

xiv. 施肇基, "修改條約事," August 1925, 03-16-043-02-011, JSSDAG / 北洋政府外交部; 施肇基, "修正條約事," July 1925, 03-16-043-02-002, JSSDAG / 北洋政府外交部; 施肇基, "取消不平等條約

事," June 1925, 03-23-019-02-004, JSSDAG / 北洋政府外交部; 施肇基, "關於修改不平等條約事," June 1925, 03-23-102-03-002, JSSDAG / 北洋政府外交部.

xv.   BCA, 434A1, 30..10.0.0, 257.728..1., (30 November 1926)

xvi.   施肇基, "游歷土耳其感想," 13.

xvii. 汉民, "就土耳其革命告我国军人," 民报, 1910.

xviii. "MR. HU HAN-MING ON NEW MODEL," *The North - China Herald and Supreme Court & Consular Gazette*, 1928.

xix.   "HU HAN-MING WELCOMED BACK," *The North - China Herald and Supreme Court & Consular Gazette*, 1928.

xx.   "胡漢民談土耳其之近狀," 北平特別市公安局政治训练部旬刊, 1928.

xxi.   胡汉民(述), and 张振之(記), "考察新土耳其的經過和感想," 新亚细亚, 1930.

xxii. "Çin Hükümeti Dün Şehrimize Geldi," *Milliyet*, March 16, 1928.

xxiii. "Çin Heyeti Dün şehrimize Geldi," *Vakit Newspaper*, March 16, 1928.

xxiv. "Milli Çin Heyeti Şehrimize Geldi," *Cumhuriyet Newspaper*, March 16, 1928.

xxv.   王會善, 世界遊記選 (上海友好书店印行, 1937), 120–129.

xxvi. 賀耀組, "土耳其之建設與三民主義," 外部周刊, 1936.

xxvii. "使領館消息：駐土耳其公使賀耀組呈遞國書時前往總統府之情形：[照片]," 外部周刊, 1935.

xxvii. 郭豫才, "胡石青先生年谱," 再生, 1943.

xxviii.胡石青, "人类主义初草," 南开周刊, 1925.

xxix. 胡石青, 三十八国游记 (开封开明印刷局, 1933).

xxx.   胡石青, "遊土耳基日記," 新国家,

About the Editor and Translator

Giray Fidan is a Professor in the Chinese Translation and Interpreting Department at Haci Bayram Veli University in Ankara. He studied Sinology at Ankara University, Beijing Language and Culture University, and the Min Zu University of China and spent a year conducting research at Princeton University as a visiting scholar. His research interests are Sino-Turkish relations, Chinese-Near Eastern relations, and Chinese perceptions of Ottoman and Republican Turkey from the 15th through the 20th centuries. He has published a number of books and articles on these topics, including *Ottoman Firearms and Ottomans in China during the Kanuni Era* (2011), *Kaimo'er: The First Biography of Atatürk Published in China* (2018) (both in Turkish), and *Chinese Witness of the Young Turk Revolution: Kang Youwei's Turk Travelogue* (2019) (in English).